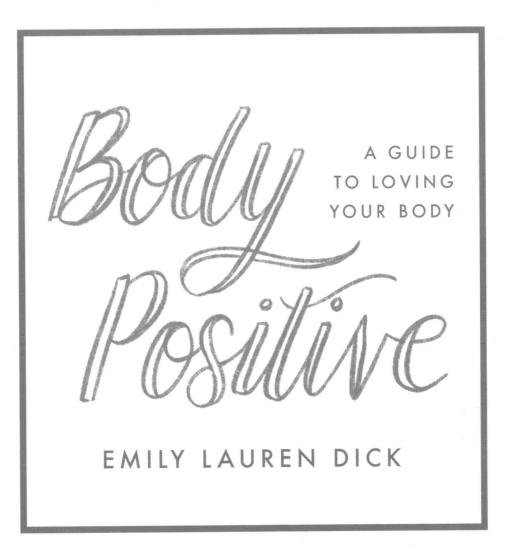

Body Positive

A GUIDE
TO LOVING
YOUR BODY

EMILY LAUREN DICK

FAMILIUS

Published by Familius LLC, www.familius.com
1254 Commerce Way, Sanger, CA 93657

Familius books are available at special discounts for bulk purchases, whether
for sales promotions or for family or corporate use. For more information,
contact Familius Sales at 559-876-2170 or email orders@familius.com.

Library of Congress Control Number: 2020941605

Print ISBN 9781641702676
Ebook ISBN 9781641703734
KF 9781641703970
FE 9781641704212

Printed in China

Edited by Laurie Duersch, Ashlin Awerkamp, and Peg Sandkam
Cover and book design by Mara Harris

10 9 8 7 6 5 4 3 2 1

First Edition

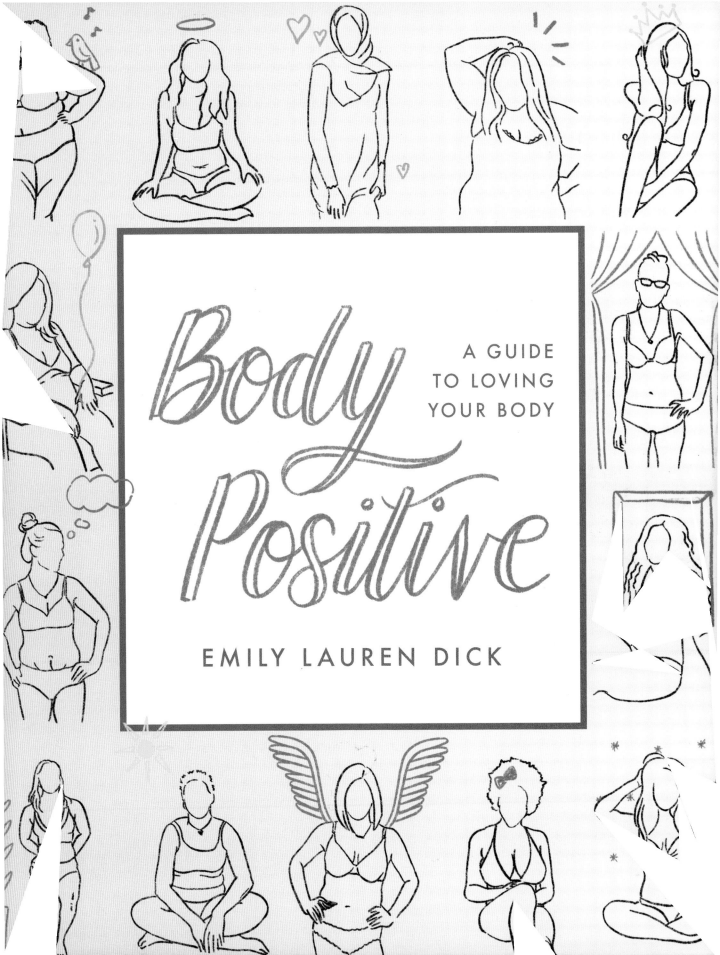

Body Positive

A GUIDE TO LOVING YOUR BODY

EMILY LAUREN DICK

CREDITS

· · · · · · · · · · · · · · · · · ·

Written and photographed by Emily Lauren Dick.

Hair and makeup by Jessica Camboia, Carmela Reina-Leonov, Alyssa McCarthy, and participants.

No Photoshop techniques (such as liquify and skin retouching) were used on the images of the women photographed. Only background and lighting adjustments were made.

The information in this book is general and should not replace evaluation and treatment by a qualified professional.

DEDICATION

This book is dedicated to every young girl out there struggling to love her body, and to all the brave young women who were photographed and interviewed for this book.

To my friend and co-driving force behind this project, Jess. Without you, none of this would have been possible. Thank you for getting this project to the next level, for keeping me motivated, for your time and skills, and for your friendship.

This book is also dedicated to my family and my children.

Kids, thank you for sharing some of your mommy time with this project. Garrett, my firstborn, thank you for helping me accept and appreciate my body more than I ever have before. Audrey, my little lady, I hope that when you grow up, you will not have to face the same pressures that exist today. I love you both with all my heart.

Graham, my husband, thank you for putting up with all my crazy and not-so-crazy ideas. Thank you for never telling me I could not do something (because you know I would just do it anyway) and for accepting all the hours I've spent making this project a reality. You have helped me become the strongest version of myself!

To my dad, who provided me with his entrepreneurial spirit and drive to create my own change.

To my mom, who never once made a negative comment about my body. Without your love and support, I would not have had the perseverance to love myself as I am.

Thank you all for believing in me!

average: ordinary, common, or normal; sometimes used to mean mediocre or inferior
Average Girl: a normal girl who has felt mediocre and who struggles with not being considered ideal by societal standards.

An Average Girl represents all girls who feel their bodies don't fit into society's standards but who are, nonetheless, unique.

CONTENTS

INTRODUCTION

> "A woman is often measured by the things she cannot control. She is measured by the way her body curves or doesn't curve, by where she is flat or straight or round. She is measured by 36-24-36 and inches and ages and numbers, by all the outside things that don't ever add up to who she is on the inside. And so if a woman is to be measured, let her be measured by the things she can control, by who she is and who she is trying to become. Because as every woman knows, measurements are only statistics. And statistics lie."
>
> —*Marilyn Monroe*

It's not easy being a girl today. We live in a culture in which Average Girls feel bad about themselves for being unable to achieve society's ideal standards of beauty. The media makes it nearly impossible for girls to develop a positive body image. Many of you may feel alone in your struggle with your body image. But you should know that your experience is . . . well, average.

Personally, I've never been a fat girl, and I've never been a skinny girl. I've always been just an Average Girl. I'm not a celebrity or a model, and I'm not a doctor or a professional athlete.

I am your everyday Average Girl taking a stand against the serious issue of body dissatisfaction.

I became a body image expert because I have been affected by the challenges of having a poor body image my whole life. I have studied it, I have lived it, and now, I want to change it.

I wrote this book to help girls understand the role
the media plays in creating and perpetuating
unattainable standards.

The cycle is hard to break, and it makes being a girl that much harder. This is the reason we need to come together and talk about our experiences. I believe that our shared stories can help pave the way to new methods of thinking and understanding.

In each chapter, I discuss a crucial issue that girls today face. In each chapter's "Getting to Know You" section, I provide some questions for you to ask yourself and reflect on. Feel free to write directly in this book in the provided spaces, or use a personal journal if that feels more comfortable. The "Chapter at a Glance" section is a summary of the important points made in the chapter. And finally, the "Average Girls" section features real girls' opinions and observations about the chapter subject. In putting together this book, I asked several girls to talk about their experiences. These are their thoughts, in their own words. (Some names have been changed.)

Every chapter includes images of real Average Girls because I believe that by seeing photographs of happy girls embracing their bodies, we can begin to celebrate all the markers of living life—scars, stretch marks, skin rolls, blemishes, bruises, and all.

My own experiences have led me to write and photograph this book for you, the Average Girl, in hopes that it will help you learn to love yourself and your average body. I hope you enjoy your journey of learning to *love average*.

"I love the fact that I always try to make everyone happy."

—LAURI (ANGEL) HILL

Chapter 1
BODY IMAGE AND LEARNING THE WAY

What is body image? Simply put, it is your idea of how others see your body. We develop certain feelings about our own bodies when we *internalize* the expectations of society. This means that we take society's ideas and attitudes about what we should look like and then make them an important part of our own identity.

Where do these societal expectations come from? An influential group, such as the media, comes up with a set of ideas and ideals, or an *ideology*, and then teaches those ideals to the rest of society in ways that may be hard to recognize. The group subtly alters people's values and attitudes to promote their objective until, eventually, society comes to believe that set of ideas as common sense. Our culture today favors thinness and beauty. This ideology has been developed by the media (whose objective is to sell us products), and it influences our society, which in turn reinforces, supports, and encourages the ideology.

> Our society's current beauty ideals, or ideas of perfection, are impossible to achieve.

As a result, many girls feel as if they have failed in some way and end up disappointed with themselves and dissatisfied with their own bodies. Some males experience a similar kind of dissatisfaction with themselves, but this book will focus on the intense negative feelings that females experience, which are largely due to the way women are represented in the media.

Media generally refers to movies, television, music, the internet, and the news, as well as advertisements or commercials that appear on television, on the internet, and in magazines. In the media, women are all too often shown as objects of male desire; men are portrayed as "viewers" who watch and judge female beauty. The media shows us all different types and sizes of men, but this is not the case for women—especially when it comes to size.

> The problem is that society has come to view this lack of diversity in size as normal.

In truth, when those with larger female bodies are represented, they tend to be portrayed as the funny, fat friend instead of the lead role. It is a disappointing stereotype all too often seen in the media.

Imagine a beautiful woman. Describe her: What is she wearing? What is she doing? What does she look like? Chances are that most of you did *not* think of yourselves. In fact, when asked what makes a woman beautiful, most of the girls who participated in the writing of this book said they didn't think of themselves as physically beautiful. Their responses alone tell us that girls have been affected by society's distorted idea of beauty. But these girls' feelings are not unique.

> A study conducted by Dove found that "only 11 percent of girls globally are comfortable describing themselves as 'beautiful.'"

When you pictured a beautiful woman a moment ago, what physical characteristics did you see? Flawless white skin and a perfect complexion, perhaps? Is she able-bodied? Does she have long hair, long legs, long eyelashes, big breasts, a small waist, and slim thighs? Maybe you imagined an air of sexiness. But what about happiness?

Unfortunately, the message of the media is that you're expected to fit into standards that are very narrow—quite literally. In the last thirty years especially, the media has significantly focused on the thinness of women. This focus is partly due to the popularity of using photo-editing software—such as Photoshop—in advertising. This software allows advertisers to alter the physical features of women in photos so they appear even more impossibly thin and flawless. The media leads you to believe that your worth depends on the way you look rather than on all the other characteristics that make you valuable.

Girls develop body issues early on in their lives due to a multitude of influences, including various forms of media.

The influence of the media creates body dissatisfaction in girls as young as age six. According to Dr. Blye Frank from Dalhousie University, "the challenges that a 14-year-old girl faced 20 years ago are the challenges faced by 9-year-old girls today." We need to examine why these body issues are developing at such young ages and put a stop to it.

One of the earliest types of media products we're exposed to is toys. These have a significant role in the construction of our identities. When we play with toys as children, we are learning certain roles and behaviors we will have in our adult lives. Girls are given toys, such as dolls, that can teach them how to act and how to look in society. Unfortunately, what some toys teach is quite negative.

For example, Mattel's Barbie is a popular doll that most of you played with while growing up. Barbie dolls teach you that in order to be considered beautiful, you need to *look* like Barbie. But many fail to realize that no human being could possibly look just like Barbie, because she is simply a plastic fantasy. Barbie dolls are often thought of as harmless toys, but the truth is that they are objects that promote dissatisfaction with one's own body. In fact, a study found that girls who were exposed to Barbie dolls had low self-esteem and wanted to be thinner.

Just playing with these dolls gives us unrealistic ideals of beauty and thinness.

IF BARBIE WERE REAL:

- Her proportions would match those of only 1 in 100,000 women.

- She would be 5 feet 9 inches tall and weigh only 110 pounds. Barbie would fit the criteria for anorexia as her BMI calculation would put her in the category of severely underweight. To put this into perspective, the minimum weight for this height is at least 145 pounds. (Although BMI is arguably now a medically incorrect and outdated way to measure a person's health.)

- Her shoe size would be a 3.

- She would not be able to menstruate.

- She would be too thin to support her upper body weight and would need to walk on all fours.

- She would be too thin to have a healthy liver or bowel system and would suffer from chronic diarrhea.

- She would eventually die of malnutrition.

Manufacturers of toys like Barbie have started to make some positive changes, such as releasing versions of the doll that are slightly curvier and more diverse. While this addition is a step in the right direction, these Barbie dolls are only slightly larger versions of the original. It should also be mentioned that the unrealistic body type of Barbie is still sold, which questions whether the new line of Barbie is an actual significant step forward in creating body-positive changes.

Not only Barbie's proportions but also what she wears can contribute to how you feel about your own body. Barbie, along with many dolls, dresses in clothing like thigh-high boots and miniskirts. This kind of clothing on dolls teaches that women should dress in clothes that are sexually appealing. The damaging and untrue message is that a woman's ultimate achievement and goal is to be sexually attractive and to receive male affection. Regardless of how you choose to dress, it's important for you to understand where these ideals are developed. Surrounding young girls with toys that promote a body-positive message would be more beneficial and would assist in negating the long-term effects of playing with toys like Barbie.

Unfortunately, many beauty and fashion products also promote the sexualization of young girls. At a time when the body and self-esteem are still developing, it's unhealthy for young girls to be too concerned with appearance or weight. And yet, inappropriate products such as thongs, hair extensions, and makeup are targeting young girls. The market's unsuitable messages toward girls are incredibly harmful to the development of healthy body image and self-esteem.

Another factor in how body image develops comes from female role models, including mothers. A role model is someone whose behavior you want to mimic, so hopefully the female role models in your life are careful about what they say about their own bodies.

> Even if you do not feel body positive, strive to be body neutral. It's important for you to try to be a good example for the young girls in your life.

Role models ought to nurture self-esteem rather than focus on physical standards.

Here are some examples of things a role model should do:

- Avoid negative statements about body weight, size, or shape.

- Compliment non-physical achievements and efforts.

- Don't talk about dieting but do talk about healthy eating.

- Talk about what she likes—not what she doesn't like—about her own body and others' bodies.

The pressure placed on us by the media and by society to achieve beauty ideals is extreme, so it's important for us all to help each other develop healthy levels of self-esteem.

Getting to Know You

Now it's time to ask yourself some questions and reflect on those answers. Fill in your responses in the provided spaces, or use a personal journal. Be open and honest with yourself. Don't be afraid to explore your thoughts, no matter how delicate or personal they may feel. This is the time for you to recognize your own beauty and learn about yourself.

What are your thoughts and feelings about your body? What is your favorite part of your body?

_____

_____

_____

_____

_____

_____

_____

List some things that might affect someone's body image.

_____

_____

_____

_____

_____

_____

Chapter at a Glance

- *Body image* is your idea of how others see your body.

- Society teaches what is considered ideal.

- Society promotes a culture of thinness.

- Current ideals of beauty and thinness are impossible to achieve and lead to our feeling disappointed in ourselves.

- One of the first forms of media we experience as children is toys. Many toys reinforce ideals of beauty and thinness.

- Barbie is not proportional to an Average Girl.

- Marketing tactics target girls with products they are too young for.

- It is important to find and be a role model who nurtures self-esteem and doesn't focus on physical standards.

- Women should encourage other women and girls to speak more positively about themselves and others.

Average Girls: Thoughts from *Real* Girls on Body Image and Learning the Way

"I mostly learned about female beauty from the media—television, magazines—and friends."

—*Gera*

"I like my waist because it's small, and I like my legs because they're sort of thin. I *hate* my arms. They're so huge and chubby. I like that I'm outgoing and bubbly."

—*Kate*

"I'm afraid of getting really fat and I'm afraid that people will think I'm disgusting if I do."

—*Stephanie*

"What makes me feel beautiful is when I feel skinny—which is not often. I feel good about myself after I've exercised. What I like about my body is my hair, my eyes, and my teeth and mouth. What I like about my personality is that I am humorous, outgoing, kind, and caring."

—*Amanda*

"A beautiful woman has a flat stomach, big boobs, skinny legs, huge eyelashes, big eyes, and plump lips. With lots of makeup! I learned that from television, magazines, and the internet."

—*Tanya*

"I wish I were smaller from the waist down."

—*Jennifer*

"A beautiful woman is a woman who is confident with her natural beauty. I think real beauty shines through personality. But if I had to list physical traits which society deems beautiful, they would definitely be everything in proportion and skinny, clear skin, long hair, and a sexy body. This is all according to men's views, obviously. I think being skinny, though, is considered most important."

—*Lily*

"Beautiful women have long hair, are skinny, are waxed or shaved, and have soft characteristics. I learned this from magazines and television."

—*Erika*

"Society's ideal characteristics of a beautiful woman are being thin, having a perfectly proportioned body (whatever that is), always looking good, keeping your opinions to yourself, and taking up as little space as possible. I learned about female beauty through magazines, advertisements, friends, television, and just the culture all around me. I've always tried to make myself beautiful by wearing makeup and clothes that show my figure, and by always trying to be thin."

—*Heidi*

"Being disgustingly thin makes me feel beautiful. I like being able to feel my bones protrude from underneath my skin. I like the fact that I don't care what others think of me."

—*Ashton*

"I learned about female beauty through life experience. I sometimes feel self-conscious about how people perceive me, because I like to be everyone's friend."

—*Chrissy*

"The media needs to really support different looks, shapes, and sizes rather than the generic Barbie type."

—*Arielle*

"Everything has been sex[ified]. Sex, sex, sex is everywhere, shoved in people's faces, so that true worth is no longer recognized unless you look like Megan Fox. Sad."

—*Melanie*

"The polarization of the media's idea of male and female bodies causes a lack of variety in commonly accepted body types for both sexes. Guys with large hips and a small waist will have as much difficulty as girls with large shoulders and small breasts in finding form-fitting clothes. If you are male, you are either manly (considered good) or effeminate (considered bad). With females, you can either be a butch or a lady. You need to give an image of something people admire or want to emulate. Real healthy and fit bodies should be used in advertising."

—*Laura*

"I am thin, but still don't feel thin enough sometimes. But then I think, why would I want one of those bikini bodies anyway? I don't like wearing skimpy bikinis. So best be happy with the body I have."

—*Kristen*

"I couldn't consider myself similar to the many models of beauty I had back then, such as Barbie and the princesses. This became another reason for my dissatisfaction with my body. But when I entered adolescence, things got worse.

"My hormones started working and my body changed completely in a way that I considered awful. I didn't change my diet, so I started gaining weight and couldn't stop the process. I'm still fighting against it. . . . When I was about thirteen I already had the body of a woman—and worse, I was seen as one. Also, cellulite and stretch marks started popping up everywhere.

"Basically, all of this was throwing a punch at whatever confidence or self-esteem I had about my body back then, which wasn't much. . . . This affected how I dressed and how I behaved. I started using clothes that showed less skin and that hid my curves and figure. . . . I avoided and still avoid any situation in which I have to wear a bikini. Buying clothes became worse and worse over the years, and I rarely felt satisfied with what I was wearing."

—*Vitoria*

"To me, a beautiful woman is someone who is good-looking and good-hearted. A great personality with a body and a face to match."

—*Samantha*

"I hate my body—no ifs, ands, or buts. But it gets me from A to B."

—*Tammy*

"I rarely feel beautiful. I like nothing about my body. I do like most of my personality."

—*Tina*

"I am proud to be
a special gift in a
short package."

—MADISON GIRARD

"I guess I learned about beauty from looking at pictures of people. I would see models who were stunning, and regular girls who were *beautiful* just because of their smiles and a light in their eyes."

—*Cupcake*

"We are told by the media that there is only one way we should look, and that's a perfect hourglass figure, with perfect hair, perfect skin, perky boobs, and perfect abs. It's unrealistic and unfair to expect that of women. When they do look like that, they're called fake, and if they're not that, they're called ugly. Woman can't win in our society; we will always be wrong—either too fat or too skinny, too fake, too slutty, too prude[y], too bitchy, too nice. . . . We're always too something.

"Women need to show each other, and men, that we all come in different shapes, colors, and sizes, with minds of our own, and that's okay. We don't have to look like supermodels. We don't have to look like Marilyn Monroe. We can have small breasts or large breasts—and both are absolutely, perfectly fine. We can be ourselves and not be judged for it or accused of wrongdoing. I don't like anything about myself."

—*Leesha*

"I have known girls who I thought were attractive, but once I got to know them, I realized how unattractive they really were! There is much more to beauty than looks."

—*Megan*

"Being told I look gorgeous makes me feel beautiful. It's just a sense of assuredness and security—not that I'm vain or anything."

—*Sahar*

"I'd always had this idea of what would make me pretty. Obviously, things like acne-free skin help, especially in your teenage years. But then I realized that even if I lost twenty pounds, I wouldn't ever be a size 0. I wouldn't ever be one of those girls who have . . . [a] gap between their thighs when they stand up. I think that even if I lost twenty pounds, I'd still be a size 12. Striving to be like the girl in magazines just wasn't realistic."

—Sophie

"I personally believe that a beautiful woman is somebody who is healthy and confident about her image and doesn't care at all what other people think about it. Also, someone who is intelligent and helpful and just a good person. But I know that society doesn't accept those people as 'beautiful.'

"They want stick-thin with a big butt and breasts. They want blonde and tall and blue eyes. Perfect nose, face not too long or round. Hair must be super long. Must be tan all the time, but not too tan. You have to be petite too. You have to have curves, but you can't be too curvy, whatever that means. You also have to have no hair on your body, other than your eyebrows and scalp. I learned about my version of female beauty through observing women and what I felt about them (i.e., wanting to emulate them, but not in an 'I look exactly like them' way). I learned about society's standards through the media."

—Alexa

Chapter 2
THE MEDIA

Because we are constantly exposed to idealistic body images in the media, we (as girls of all ages) become especially critical of ourselves. Unrealistic images appear in virtually every form of media, including advertising, television, music (videos and lyrics), magazines, video games, and the internet. A mere 5 percent of North American females have the type of body portrayed in the media. Furthermore, most of these images are manipulated by computer software. The media profits from making you feel insecure about your looks. They maintain ideologies of thinness and beauty so that insecure female consumers will purchase products that promise to help them achieve ideal bodies and beauty.

For the media, developing insecurity in girls equals profit.

Sadly, these ideologies are upheld and strengthened when society supports the notion that women are no more than the objects of heterosexual male desire. Women in the media are almost always presented as "ornaments" whose primary function is to be attractive. Even intelligent women need to be beautiful to be considered valuable to society. Just look at your local news station for proof that sexiness is an equally, if not more, important prerequisite than intelligence. In fact, if an intelligent woman has something to say, the media almost always finds a way to make her credibility about her appearance rather than her goals or achievements. Another example of society presenting women as objects of desire is how the media frequently discusses the clothing choices of women in politics over their male counterparts.

This sometimes subtle message instills in women the idea that the desire men feel depends on whether a woman has achieved physical beauty. Women are taught that they must be sexually attractive in order to attract mates, and in turn, men are taught that they need to get a sexually attractive mate in order to be seen as masculine and successful. Ultimately, these attitudes can promote feelings of inferiority in heterosexual females and superiority in heterosexual males. These feelings allow the media to achieve the profit they aim for.

Only a tiny percentage of real women's bodies resemble the body types of models and celebrities. And yet, the media values only those who fit this "ideal" image. The media's portrayal of women inaccurately suggests that thinness and success are related, which might lead women to believe that thinness is *equal* to success. Women are left with the false idea that achieving ideal beauty will provide them with power and the means to be successful. However, in reality, success is determined by many factors unrelated to ideal beauty.

If you haven't felt it already, the pressure to be thin and beautiful is increasing. In her book *The Beauty Myth*, Naomi Wolf explains that,

> "a generation ago [approximately the 1970s], the average model weighed 8 percent less than the average American woman, whereas today [the 1990s] she weighs 23 percent less."

To make you buy in to its ideologies, the media creates popular culture (such as music, fashion, and entertainment) to stimulate *you*, the female audience. Those behind the media know that this pop culture has to be pleasurable as well as ideological. The media takes advantage of your enjoyment and hides its ideologies of beauty and thinness behind entertainment. What this means, unfortunately, is that images in the media don't just tell us about typical female interests like fashion but also tell us how we should act and what we should look like, discouraging us from seeking any alternatives.

> "A culture fixated on female thinness is not an obsession about female beauty, but an obsession about female obedience."
>
> —*Naomi Wolf*

We can see that "a whole media industry has developed around fueling body dissatisfaction." According to the Media Awareness Network, advertisers know that females who are insecure about their bodies are more likely to buy beauty products, clothing, and dieting plans. Women who view mass media images are at more risk of developing a negative body image, eating disorders, and, consequently, depression. A Dove study found that "looking at magazines for just 60 minutes lowers self-esteem in over 80% of girls."

> On top of lowering self-esteem, messages in the media teach that being thin and beautiful is the same as being healthy, which is not true.

They also make us forget the many factors that make it hard for us to achieve today's body and beauty ideals, such as our genes, which is the set of instructions in our cells that determines what we look like and how our bodies respond to the environment.

One thing many girls don't realize is that the images of celebrities and models we see in magazines, videos, and on the internet have been manipulated to create a look that is impossible to achieve. Photoshop is one software program that can alter any image to look a particular way. With just a few clicks of the mouse or the selection of a filter, anyone can change a photo so that a woman has a thinner waist, larger breasts, or perfect skin.

> These manipulated images are especially dangerous because they reinforce unrealistic and unachievable standards.

In the past, what set models apart was having genes that made them taller and more symmetrical, along with professional makeup and lighting. Today, Photoshop and apps with filters can manipulate anyone's looks.

When the media manipulates images of women, they also manipulate our idea of what an Average Girl or Woman really looks like. Our society needs to take a step back and start demanding images with positive messages about beauty that challenge the media's agendas. Without images of real, average bodies, we can't repair the damage done by current media imagery. The ideologies that are currently popular may not go down without a fight, so we have to develop and support body-positive images that help girls question what the media is actually promoting. The more educated we are about the media's unrealistic representations of women, the better equipped we are to battle this ideology.

It is especially important to note that while we do need to learn to be critical of the media's messages, you should not feel guilty for enjoying the entertainment that media sources provide. Although it may seem prudent to cut out these influences entirely, doing so is not realistic. Rather than simply condemning all media, we must educate ourselves about how women are represented. Our goal is to challenge any media that promotes body dissatisfaction, not to stop women from enjoying it.

Getting to Know You

Now it's time to ask yourself some questions and reflect on those answers. Fill in your responses in the provided spaces, or use a personal journal. Be open and honest with yourself. Don't be afraid to explore your thoughts, no matter how delicate or personal they may feel. This is the time for you to recognize your own beauty and learn about yourself.

Describe the body type you see most often in magazines, on television, and in the movies.

_____

_____

_____

_____

_____

_____

_____

_____

_____

_____

_____

_____

_____

Why do you think this body type is favored in the media?

_____

_____

_____

_____

_____

_____

_____

_____

_____

Why do you think advertising companies alter images of women rather than leaving them as they are?

_____

_____

_____

_____

_____

_____

_____

_____

_____

"I think if we can start showing girls early that you don't have to be 'thin' or 'perfect' to be beautiful we can accomplish truly great things."

—LYNN BRUBACHER

Chapter at a Glance

- Women are taught from a young age that they need to achieve idealistic standards of beauty in order to attract heterosexual men.

- The media invented ideologies of thinness and beauty so they could generate insecurity and body dissatisfaction in women.

- Only 5 percent of women have the body type commonly portrayed in the media.

- Most images of women in the media are altered to make them look thinner and supposedly more beautiful.

- The pleasure and enjoyment we get from entertaining media mask its damaging ideologies, which encourage us to buy products we think will help us achieve ideals of thinness and beauty.

- We need alternative forms of media that promote average bodies of all kinds.

"ALL women are beautiful and that there is no one type of women that is perfect and that should be praised as beautiful."

—ZAINA HUSSAIN

Average Girls: Thoughts from *Real* Girls on the Media

"Most girls have curves, but people promote skinny as better."

—*Kay*

"The media pressures girls of *all* ages to be perfect and cool-looking, from having the newest Barbie when they're young to having the perfect everything when they [are] elementary-school age and older. It's ridiculous because people get teased . . . about their appearance—not even their personality, but their *appearance*—and it's so hard not to get wrapped into it. People usually do. I know I do."

—*Madeleine*

"The media is the biggest reason for my being anorexic."

—*Alli*

"Perfect skin, long eyelashes, big eyes, pink lips . . . I don't know, I just think it's pretty. That's always shown in films and in magazines and stuff. I just love the look I can't do. I'm just ugly, and I can't be [bothered] to do makeup—don't have much money for makeup anyway."

—*Monica*

"The struggle for teen girls to look like someone they're not is real. They are surrounded by it every day on magazine covers showing singers, actresses, etc."

—*Sahar*

"I think models seem too skinny, but when you look at the modern ideal for figures, it's not necessarily the runway you look at but movies, television shows, music videos, daily life. Women like Kim Kardashian, J. Lo, and various Playboy models are seen as most desirable and attractive when it comes to body type."

—Dalton

"The media creates the problem and then offers the solution."

—Sara

"The media is the world's worst [culprit] about making it impossible for us to just live. They are the ones who determine what is 'normal' and that you are not it, and all the ways that you should be singled out for torture by the masses."

—Tammy

"The media definitely had a key role in the construction of my beauty ideals and, consequently, the problems I have with my body image. When you don't see beauty models who look like you, you start to feel like there is something wrong with you. The media doesn't show diversity, but oftentimes criticizes it."

—Vitoria

"The media sucks. People are easily influenced by it. It's all about being as thin as you can and having the latest trend. And then people moan when girls are anorexic."

—Lauren

"The media does *not* help in portraying a healthy image to little girls of how a woman should look. All these famous celebrities that preteens and teens look up to (like Miley Cyrus, Selena Gomez, Cher Lloyd) are all *so* thin, and it makes girls think that everyone has to be thin if they want to be popular. Some people say that the media has little to do with eating disorders, but I think that the media plays a huge part in the onset of eating disorders."

—*Kate*

"If consumers of media look for perfection and that perfection is an ideal of something that is unattainable or the epitome of disordered eating or unhealthy practices, then it becomes normalized and easier to justify that you don't have a problem when . . . you do. I used the media to justify the fact that I was fine when, in fact, I should have been hospitalized."

—*Leonie*

"Girls, as well as boys, see the media's images as 'perfection.' With unrealistic images, no one will ever be happy with their own image or the partner they're with."

—*Rae*

"The enhanced images we see on the glossy pages of magazines and scattered across advertising is skewing girls' perceptions of what women actually look like. This gives them an unrealistic expectation of how they want themselves to look and is pretty much asking for them to feel like a failure, as they'll never look like the women in the magazines."

—*Claira*

"I hate how society or the media . . . are applauded if they do anything with someone who is bigger than a size 2."

—*Sasha*

"Models and celebrities are bad examples to compare yourself to. I usually compare myself to people I see around town and at school. A model's job is to look good; they need to maintain 'perfection' so they don't lose their job. It's not realistic to compare yourself to them."

—*Pearl*

"I wish the media could be sued for misrepresenting the true female body."

—*Lina*

"Skinny, Photoshopped women are *everywhere* on the internet, where most people spend their day. Couple this with beauty standards, and gendered norms *no one* could keep up with, and you have the perfect storm of eating disorders and depression, both of which reinforce each other. I think we're getting to the point with dieting, eating disorders, and depression where society can't ignore them anymore. They're too widespread, too big, too loud to be ignored. People are speaking up, women especially, and they are fed up. It's time for a change."

—*Kat*

"The media puts too much emphasis on being thin. Women of all sizes can be beautiful."

—*Morgan*

"If I see one more 'bikini challenge' advertisement, I will punch the computer! I want to scream at all my friends who like them and tell them to stop poisoning their minds! But yes, I am guilty. I have spent years comparing models' bodies and liking things like that, but have recently had a magazine clean-out.

"I think the women in the media are also real women. They are all just as subject to the comparisons and expectations of society, so we can't discredit them. It hurts to be called fat; it also hurts to be called a runt. But maybe [the media] could show *all* women, in their natural state—no airbrushing, no lighting, no makeup, no scenery, etc.— just doing normal things in their normal lives that we can relate to."

—*Louise*

"I love the idea of taking Photoshop out of advertising. It's not so much erasing a random pimple or improving someone's complexion, but the manipulation of women's bodies that is way out of control. If girls could see women in the media without the manipulation, they would have a more realistic idea of how their own bodies develop instead of striving for an impossible goal."

—*Kimberly*

"I am very involved in feminism. It took a long time to unlearn the Victoria's Secret standard of beauty and learn a more important one."

—*Hanna*

"The media is to blame for why we think we have to be skinny to be beautiful. . . . We need more media supporting full-figured and average-sized women."

—*Kayla*

"This is
what I'm
supposed
to look
like after a
mastectomy
and it's
totally fine."

—MELANIE HICKS

"Fashion models are fantasy figures and fashion is a form of art. I think you can use very beautiful models of all sizes and have more truth in editing. All women are real, thin or not. But we can stop airbrushing skin to the appearance of smooth vinyl plastic and maybe let a flaw sneak in here or there. I mean come on, moles and freckles aren't imperfections!"

—*Michelle*

"As a teenager, I was almost obsessed with trying to be what the girls in magazines were. I was well into my twenties, after I'd had my first baby, that I began to appreciate my body for what it could do and not just what it looked like. The media and social media are tough on girls, but at least now we know about the airbrushing and Photoshopping, etc. When I was a kid, we thought they really looked that way. Kids now are more aware of the tricks."

—*Gera*

"I think media images had more of an effect on my comparing myself to celebrities when I was a teen, but since I've become an adult, I have a greater understanding of how these media images are not accurate, and they don't have the same impact on me anymore."

—*Nicole*

"We need to see all kinds of bodies in the media. Not just small ones, not just big ones, but bodies of all shapes, sizes, and colors. We need to stop telling girls that they have to look like Barbie to be attractive."

—*Stephanie*

"I learned about female beauty from fashion magazines, porn, celebrities, and the media. I grew up believing that to be a beautiful woman, you had to have a small, flat waist; huge breasts; a round bottom; long, shapely, smooth legs; small hands and feet; delicate features; and long, thick hair.

"As I've gotten older, I have stayed away from the media as much as I can, and my ideas about what makes a woman beautiful have changed slightly. A woman is beautiful when she is the right, healthy size for herself, whether that be a size 6 or a size 22. Confidence also plays a big part in it, but I believe healthy is beautiful."

—*Leesha*

"Real women are *real*. Not faked with Photoshop or airbrushing. Keep it *real*."

—*Hailey*

Chapter 3
SELF-IMPROVEMENT

Girlguiding, the leading charity for girls and young women in the UK, produces an annual survey about girls' attitudes on a variety of topics and issues. Their 2016 survey found that 15 percent of girls aged seven to ten, 54 percent of girls aged eleven to sixteen, and 66 percent of girls aged seventeen to twenty-one felt they are not pretty enough.

As girls enter their teenage years, the effects of having a negative body image increase.

> Poor body image can lead to several problems for young women, including low self-esteem, depression, eating disorders, and even being bullied.

As women, we tend to compare our bodies to the images of women in the media. Advertisers benefit from your body dissatisfaction because their messages teach and train you to seek out self-improvement measures in an attempt to fix what you have been told is wrong with you. This, in turn, increases your media consumption as you interact on social media, read magazines, watch television, and so on.

> And the result of this "'vicious circle' of media exposure" (internalizing its message, comparing and judging yourself, and consuming more media) is that your body dissatisfaction is reinforced.

According to the American Psychological Association and the Common Sense Census, "the average child or teen watches 3 hours of television per day" and spends nearly eight hours on entertainment screen media per day. (This includes phones and tablets.) It's no wonder the media has such an effect on us! "Children and adolescents spend more time with entertainment media than they do with any other activity except school and sleeping." Young women are especially at risk of internalizing the media's ideals. As they develop their identity, they are influenced by the behavior of the women they see around them, including those in the public spotlight. In place of a positive role model, the media can become one of the most influential systems in young women's lives.

According to author and filmmaker Dr. Jean Kilbourne, advertising sells us values, images, concepts of love and sexuality, success, and normalcy. It also tells us who we are supposed to be. The media pressures us into purchasing products promoted by advertisers and celebrities so that we can compete with other women. They profit off female insecurity by selling products that promise to help us achieve ideal beauty. But when, inevitably, we are unable to achieve these impossible standards, we feel bad about ourselves and go on searching for the next solution offered up by advertisers.

Each year $33 billion is spent on weight loss, and $7 billion is spent on cosmetics. Self-improvement ranges from trying the latest fad diet that promises dramatic weight loss to buying a makeup concealer that promises to hide all your imperfections. Countless so-called self-improvement strategies exist out there, and now girls start using them at a very young age. In the 1970s, the average age at which girls started to diet was fourteen. By the 1990s, it was eight.

Dieting has become a normal practice for women, especially young women. We might decide to try a diet because we believe it will help us achieve our ideal body image.

> But statistics show that the effects of dieting (or rather, disordered eating) are not long-lasting and likely lead to gaining the lost weight back.

Gaining the weight back causes us to feel even more dissatisfied and disappointed in ourselves. In fact, 98 percent of all diets fail.

But because diets sometimes cause short-term weight loss, girls are tempted to try dieting again and again. In the long run, however, this practice only creates poor self-esteem and could lead to developing an eating disorder.

Another common self-improvement process is the use of cosmetics. Cosmetics are makeup products intended to improve your appearance and confidence in a temporary way. Makeup offers something different to each person who wears it. Some wear makeup because they believe it helps them attract the opposite sex by highlighting their femininity. Others use makeup to hide what they consider imperfections. For many, makeup creates a sense of confidence, perhaps because it enhances features that society considers beautiful.

The Renfrew Center Foundation recently conducted a study of girls (aged eight to eighteen) and found that many of them wear makeup to mask their insecurities. It also found that two-thirds of the girls started wearing makeup between the ages of eight and thirteen. Adrienne Ressler, the vice president of professional development of the Renfrew Center, explained that when we start using makeup as an extension of ourselves, to literally *make up* for what we think we are lacking, it becomes a problem. The Renfrew Center sponsors a campaign called "Barefaced & Beautiful, Without & Within," which encourages women to go without makeup for a day and focus on their inner beauty. Ressler says, "The campaign isn't to denounce makeup, but to have girls and women, in particular girls, look at themselves and focus more on who they are rather than how they look."

Many of us self-improve because we feel we have to, rather than because we enjoy it.

This is proven by the fact that girls are looking for quick fixes to supposed flaws at young ages. If this is the case, we will never really be able to enjoy self-improvement.

FOR EXAMPLE:

- Dieting is no fun if you love food.

- Wearing Spanx and other fat-sucking clothing is often uncomfortable, even painful.

- Extreme diets involving laxatives, diet pills, and so on are dangerous for your health.

- Makeup should be fun and not take hours to put on.

- Cosmetic surgery (a medical procedure to permanently change the look of part of your body) is risky, painful, and expensive.

"I believe positive real bodies will also help with anxiety/ depression towards positive love for our own bodies as well."

—VICTORIA TRINH

Some of these methods of supposed self-improvement are not at all enjoyable or pleasurable, and yet people still spend billions of dollars on them every year. All of this proves one thing: People (and especially women) are being convinced that they need fixing.

As a woman (young or old), you should not be made to feel that you have to improve yourself physically in order to be happy and prosperous. How can we stop this message from going out? By demanding representations of realistic, average bodies and all their differences. The battle to get average images into mainstream media will be difficult, but it is necessary if we want to improve the physical and mental health of girls everywhere.

Getting to Know You

Now it's time to ask yourself some questions and reflect on those answers. Fill in your responses in the provided spaces, or use a personal journal. Be open and honest with yourself. Don't be afraid to explore your thoughts, no matter how delicate or personal they may feel. This is the time for you to recognize your own beauty and learn about yourself.

What are some of the things you do to make yourself feel beautiful?

_____

_____

_____

_____

_____

_____

What kinds of advertisements are particularly appealing to you?

_____

_____

_____

_____

_____

_____

Have you ever purchased something and been disappointed because it didn't work the way you expected?

_____

_____

_____

_____

_____

_____

_____

_____

_____

_____

_____

_____

_____

_____

_____

_____

_____

_____

_____

Chapter at a Glance

- The media profits off insecurity and body dissatisfaction by offering supposed solutions. These solutions cost money.

- People spend more time watching media entertainment than doing any other activity (excluding school, work, and sleep).

- The media tells girls who they are supposed to be.

- Advertisers benefit from girls feeling like they need to compete with each other.

- Self-improvement measures are intended to fix flaws. They include a variety of uncomfortable (and sometimes painful) practices, such as dieting and cosmetic surgery.

- People spend billions of dollars every year on self-improvement.

"Today, I love my body. I have gained self confidence in the past few years and I carry this confidence with me now."

—AGATHA CHOY

Average Girls: Thoughts from *Real* Girls on Self-Improvement

"The only time I truly feel better is when I'm wearing makeup."

—*Alli*

"I make myself beautiful by wearing makeup every day, wearing a padded bra, using body sprays, shaving, eyebrow plucking, occasionally straightening my hair, moisturizing . . ."

—*Leesha*

"I make myself beautiful with makeup, by curling my hair, and by wearing high heels and a dress. Diets? Done them all. Hate them. They make me feel guilty and I end up bingeing."

—*Louise*

"I don't make myself beautiful. It's impossible."

—*Leslie*

"For years I had a struggle with my weight—which I still haven't won—with not fitting into the beauty model society gives us, and at the same time, with trying to accept myself. I've made some progress with the last one, but still haven't reached the point at which I feel satisfied with my body. . . . I'm still searching for full self-acceptance though."

—*Vitoria*

"Beauty is confidence, beautiful skin (not plastic), being skinny with no cellulite, muscles that are in proportion and toned. Happiness. I learned about the female body by looking at those around me, by experimenting with my own, watching it change. I didn't know much and I didn't care about my body, so I went to every extreme to figure out what was possible to make the body do.

"I make myself beautiful by experimenting with it, changing it into what I want it to be, not someone else's idea. I make myself beautiful by being as skinny as I can. Everything else I really hate and would change if I could, and if I didn't believe it would be an act of desperation and shame [I would] actually modify my body with plastic surgery."

—*Leonie*

"Girls won't always be skinny and tan and look like teenagers—unless they're rich and can afford surgeries, or are really super healthy. And even then, you can have scars and flaws."

—*Heather*

"It's really sad. Diets are only necessary if you live off junk food and are fat as hell."

—*Monica*

"In third grade, a girl and boy in my class asked me if I was pregnant and then started to tease me about who the father was. I didn't even know how you became pregnant at the time. That's the same year my mom put my sister and me on a diet."

—*Kimberly*

"There's no one definition of beauty."

—JESSICA HENDRIKS

"I think there is a lot of pressure on women (and now men too) to diet and have their bodies look a certain way, resulting in a rise in unhealthy dieting, eating disorders, and depression. I think those who strive for this ideal end up being depressed because trying to achieve this standard is unrealistic and a full-time job, so one never has time to enjoy their life. And because the standard isn't realistic, these individuals are constantly letting themselves down and being depressed as a result.

"I think there is a lot of misinformation out there about diets, and there is a rise in fad diets (e.g., paleo, raw food, etc.). There is pressure from society that if you don't engage in one of these fad diets, you are 'bad.' It seems to greatly contribute to the all-or-nothing thinking that is largely responsible for eating disorders."

—*Nicole*

"I have been on most of the diets out there. They don't work. I've tried the whole 'eating healthy and changing the way you think' thing. It doesn't work. Our society is geared to make you fat. Fattening food is cheaper than good food and we are encouraged by everything to eat it. We can't win."

—*Tammy*

"I feel beautiful when I take care of myself by exercising and pampering my body."

—*Alanna*

"No matter what people say, we're always going to want to look like those girls in magazines."

—*Tanya*

"When I was fifteen, my mum joined a weight loss club that was about losing weight naturally. As my sister and I were chubby/fat teens, we joined as well. When I joined, I weighed 110 kilograms [242.5 pounds]. To weigh in each week, a majority of the women would strip down to their underwear to make sure that the weight of jeans, T-shirts, shoes, etc., didn't add any extra kilos or grams. I also picked up on this habit and still today, if I go to step on a scale, I will automatically strip to just my bra and underwear to weigh myself.

"I realized that this group was messing with my head when I weighed in one day—that week I'd eaten next to nothing and walked just about everywhere—and I had gained weight. I cried and cried. My mum, trying to comfort me, said, 'It's okay, at least you weigh less than when we joined.' I weighed 112 kilograms [246.9 pounds]. I was an absolute mess."

—*Pandora*

"We [pressure] each other to be better, prettier—to be more. This leads to depression and/or eating disorders. Dieting is now the whore of money."

—*Rachel*

"Many people go on diets to lose weight when they are already fit and healthy."

—*Gloria*

"I dieted on and off through middle school and high school, thinking that was what I was supposed to do. Girls spend too much time thinking about dieting and not enough time thinking about how to crush the patriarchy."

—*Jessica*

"No one should feel like their body type isn't a good body type; we all deserve to feel beautiful and have equal opportunities."

—SIERRA LEFAVE

"I have lost eighty-plus pounds in the past few years and am constantly in a state of alternately shaming myself if I go up a few pounds, and shaming myself for caring so much about how I look. It's a never-ending cycle of shame and dissatisfaction."

—*Deanna*

"Dieting shouldn't be about cutting stuff out or anything like that. It's much healthier and more effective in the long run to simply cut your portion sizes to a reasonable (not minuscule) amount and to eat healthier food."

—*Emily*

"Through life experiences, I figured out for myself what being beautiful means, and using makeup highlights my inner beauty."

—*Sahar*

Chapter 4
SELF-COMPARISON AND FAT TALK

· ·

When you compare yourself to women in the media, you are more likely to internalize the thinness ideal and have a negative body image. When you're unable to meet ideal standards, you may feel like you're not good enough.

The media makes it nearly impossible to avoid judging yourself against society's standard of beauty.

For example, if a magazine model is able-bodied with white skin, large breasts, and a tiny waist, you may compare the size of your own body, breasts, and waist to the model's and feel that you need to have the same characteristics to be considered beautiful. Ultimately, you end up feeling critical of your own body. Self-comparison (or social comparison) leads to self-criticism; in other words, you evaluate yourself and then feel that you want to correct yourself.

Often when women are unable to meet society's unattainable standards, they feel ashamed.

> "Comparison is an act of violence against the self."
> —*Iyanla Vanzant*

Shame often leads to *fat talk*, a form of negative talk about one's own body that has become a regular practice among girls. Mimi Nichter, a sociocultural anthropologist, discovered the social ritual of fat talk while studying teenage girls' eating habits and physical ideals. Fat-talk statements reinforce unattainable body and beauty ideals and have become so common that many of us don't even realize we're participating in it. Do you, for example, regularly say things like "I feel so fat today" or "She's so much prettier than I'll ever be"?

Fat talk is often used to describe our feelings about the pressures of body and beauty standards. Unfortunately, fat talk only causes us to keep feeling bad about our bodies. When we engage in fat talk, we're expressing how we feel about being unable to live up to societal standards, and we're relating to other females who feel the same. Another reason we fat talk is for reassurance. A common response to another person's fat-talk comment is "You're not fat—you're thin!" Sometimes we are simply looking for someone to tell us that it's okay not to reach for society's ideals, but this motivation is often interpreted as "fishing for compliments."

Fat talk is harmful to all women and passes unrealistic ideals down to younger generations as girls hear their mothers, older sisters, and other female role models engaging in fat talk, and then they mimic it themselves.

> It's important for us to find ways to express our true feelings—and fat is not a feeling!

Fat talk is essentially talking negatively about yourself and expressing negative feelings (like disgust) over being "fat" or feeling worthless. If you ritually tell yourself over and over that you are not good enough, those feelings will start to become part of your identity. We must understand that our wants, likes, and thoughts are deeply affected by the body image ideals we've internalized. Our responsibility as women is to start these conversations about our true feelings and remind ourselves and our fellow Average Girls that what may seem like common sense is not!

> Young women who engage in a lot of self-comparison and negative self-talk are at increased risk of developing poor self-esteem, eating disorders, and depression.

"I love everything about my body, especially my curvy hips."

—RENEE MARTINS

The good news is that studies have found a way to decrease this risk, which is to teach girls not to compare themselves to media images and to be critical of such unrealistic standards. *There is more than one acceptable body type.*

To really accept this fact, we need to see these body types positively represented in the media.

> **In a recent study, when female subjects were shown photos of larger women, their preference for thin bodies decreased; however, when they were shown images of thin women, they preferred thinness.**

If we can display alternative representations of women in the media, we can start to repair the damage of impossible ideals and change how they affect Average Girls.

"Instead of viewing
ourselves as having
"flaws," we should
view ourselves
as having
differences
that make
us unique
and special."

—BRITTANY PESTRAK

Getting to Know You

Now it's time to ask yourself some questions and reflect on those answers. Fill in your responses in the provided spaces, or use a personal journal. Be open and honest with yourself. Don't be afraid to explore your thoughts, no matter how delicate or personal they may feel. This is the time for you to recognize your own beauty and learn about yourself.

Who do you compare yourself to? Why?

_____

_____

_____

_____

_____

_____

If one of your friends or family members were making negative comments about her body, what advice could you give her to make her feel better about herself?

_____

_____

_____

_____

_____

_____

Chapter at a Glance

- Girls who feel bad about not being able to meet society's ideal standards are at increased risk of developing a negative body image.

- Comparing yourself to models, celebrities, and other girls can make you critical of yourself.

- *Fat talk* is making negative statements about one's body in everyday conversation.

- Fat talk reinforces thin ideals.

- Feelings of negativity and shame about not meeting ideal standards lead to fat talk.

- Society needs to positively accept more than one type of body.

- If more representations of average bodies were available in the media, girls would feel better about themselves.

"I'm First Nations,
Mohawk and
Onondaga nations.
I feel my culture is a
big part of who I am."

—CAITLYNN HILL

Average Girls: Thoughts from *Real* Girls on Self-Comparison and Fat Talk

"Because I want to be beautiful, I see their beauty, but all I can see are my flaws."

—*Leslie*

"The place where I really compare myself is at the gym. I love exercise, but I need to compare myself to every other woman there. It is an obsession. I compare myself to every woman I see. I have to try really hard not to do it."

—*Sam*

"Sometimes you just see someone who makes you look at yourself critically because (in your eyes) they're better than you, because they seem to get a lot of adoration based on their looks."

—*Cupcake*

"[If you have a larger body,] people think they can give you advice or that you are lazy. They have no idea of the barriers you face. Most of these people are close to you, which hurts the most. People don't appreciate you for who you really are. You're just a 'fat person' to them. Whereas I can look at people and think they are unhealthy because they live with [an] incredible amount of stress."

—*Megan*

"You shouldn't compare yourself to others, but it's hard not to."

—*Alexa*

"I think women are programmed by society to compare [them]selves to each other, to be aesthetically pleasing to men, and exist to decorate [a man's] world and bear their children. I think social media allows you to see how sexist and small-minded people can be toward women. Women call each other names and put each other down; men call women names and put them down. . . . It seems sometimes that the whole world is against women.

"I always compare myself to other women, wishing I had their waist, hair, boobs, bum. . . . Women have to have a tiny waist, huge hips and ass, and big, perky boobs. And if we don't have them, then we're 'not curvy enough' or 'not real women.' Last time I checked, real women had vaginas and their gender wasn't based on their size or shape. I try to stay away from the media as much as I can; it just makes me feel terrible about myself."

—Leesha

"I have one friend who won't even have a mirror in her house or look in a mirror to do her hair or makeup. Very sad!"

—Megan

"I've always compared myself to other girls. I feel like if I don't look like them, I'm probably not beautiful. And if I'm not as skinny or pretty as someone else, then I'm not good enough."

—Heidi

"I was a very thin and slim child. I could eat whatever I wanted and I wouldn't gain weight, so I didn't have—and still don't [have]— the healthiest diet. But at around eight, I started comparing myself to other girls. I wanted to be thinner, even though you could see my ribs."

—Vitoria

"I believe that at the root of my body image issues is the feeling of needing to attract a man. I simply do not feel good on the inside unless I feel put together on the outside. Unfortunately, if I don't feel good about my appearance, I feel unworthy of finding a relationship.

"I also struggle with the issue of comparison, as I feel that men will compare and judge me against other girls. While my concern over this has nothing to do with models or celebrities, I feel that those ideal images are what lead men to believe that women should look a specific way. I get a front-row seat to this in my social group, which is mostly men. I hear them discussing the way girls look and how they compare to unrealistic standards, but I do recognize they may be doing it because of a group mentality. The men I like most are those in relationships, because they tend to be more sensitive to my feelings and I don't feel pressured to impress or look a certain way."

—*Sara*

"It wasn't until my twenties that my body image started to be affected by the media. Before that, it was all comparison to other girls at my school."

—*Kimberly*

"With the rise of new digital platforms, the body and beauty ideals presented by the media have become a kind of urban wallpaper. We need to see more realistic ideals of beauty so we can stop comparing ourselves to something that doesn't even exist."

—*Mandy*

"I compare myself to others because, sometimes, I'd like to alter parts of my body."

—*Pearl*

"Every woman's body is beautiful no matter how many stretch marks or scars it may carry."

−TYMIKA KLOTZ

> "I find myself comparing my body to those of more attractive women."
> —Karie

"After high school, I attended college, where I studied dance. It was the most probable place for weight issues to be an everyday topic. To my recollection, I was not worried about my size or weight. In fact, I had a friend in first year who was a similar size, if not bigger than me, and we used to joke about our poor technique in ballet due to our oversized thighs. To me it was harmless. I hope it was to her too.

"A few people made mention of the fact that I had lost a bit of weight and that I looked good. It was the first time I had ever received that compliment. I started saying out loud that I knew I was fat, that what others saw (even if they didn't actually see it), I saw too. I felt better saying it out loud . . . so that whatever they were thinking wasn't so secretive. As if to say, 'Yes, I know what you're thinking. I already know. I'm working on it.'"

—Melissa

"An hourglass figure, feminine facial features like high cheekbones; full lips; a thin, cute nose; big eyes; and long eyelashes—you're born with it or you get surgery."

—Dalton

"The media and popular culture cultivate a space where we are expected to fit into a certain body type, and women are placed in constant competition with each other for the prettiness prize. But we're either too fat or too thin, or we are killing ourselves to maintain. Though I should know better, I constantly do the body comparison when I see other women I would like to model."

—Deanna

"I try not to compare myself to others, because I find that I'm the least smart, least beautiful, and least likely to get into a good college compared to most of my friends. (Take into consideration that I'm in the advanced placement section of my school, so I'm around people with a GPA over 4.0, while I'm getting a 3.07.) So overall, all of my friends are beautiful, and I'm just the nerd of the group, with glasses, to boot. I would get really depressed if I thought about these things too much, but I don't. So I'm okay with how I look, for now."

—Erika

"It's sad that we compare ourselves, but it's also like a hobby. It gives me something to think about. It sometimes makes me happy to browse through pretty clothes that others have. But other times, I feel a little upset that I can't afford them, or I'm too ugly to wear them."

—Monica

"I only compare myself to others when I'm in a non-thinking state. It's female nature to do this!"

—Heaven

"It would be more bearable to have something realistic to compare ourselves to (if we must)."

—Deanna

"We're going to compare ourselves anyway; we might as well compare ourselves to actual people!"

—Genni

"The media is a double-edged sword. It can be a useful tool for education and information. But often the pressure on the media to generate audiences and commercial interests will lead to sensationalizing. It is neither bad nor good, but people have to use common sense in judging what information they believe and what they should censor for themselves."

—*Sandra*

"I'm fine unless I'm feeling ugly. Then I'm all about observing beautiful people and comparing myself to them . . . and making myself feel so much worse."

—*Danielle*

"I've always been heavy. It took me a long time to honestly say that I loved myself. I loved seeing my friends in these super cute outfits and I wished I could wear those clothes too. But when you're a size 20 in the seventh grade, those clothes aren't even *near* your section of the store.

"I suppose I compared myself to them then, but I let it go when I hit high school. I realized that wanting to be thin and actually *being* thin were two different things. I was just making myself miserable. I had to work with what I had. I learned to love myself because I knew I wasn't going to change my weight overnight. I started to dress for my shape and it seemed to work for me."

—*Erin*

Chapter 5
THINSPIRATION

*T*hinspiration, or "thinspo," is one of the newest phenomena that pressure girls today. Thinspiration is the use of images, along with slogans or quotes, to inspire women to lose weight through dieting or exercise to attain a thin body ideal. *Fitspiration* is a similar practice intended to inspire women to do punishing exercise to attain a fit body ideal. These practices promote extreme thinness as attractive.

Many of the images used for thinspiration are the same kind of thing you see in the media on a regular basis. Photos of models and celebrities are commonly used to represent the ultimate goal of thinness, although regular girls are used as well. They are usually shown in their underwear, bathing suits, or barely there (nearly nude) clothing. Sometimes the image is of only a body part rather than the whole body.

> What's disturbing is that thinspiration images often depict bodies that are skinny to an unhealthy extreme.

These images glorify protruding ribs, hollowed-out stomachs, and skeletal frames. Furthermore, some of these photos have been manipulated with Photoshop in the same way mainstream advertisements are.

Another kind of thinspiration is created by using images of women who represent the opposite of thin as a scare tactic. Images of "fat" girls are matched with demeaning and hurtful messages meant to scare the viewer into doing whatever they can to avoid looking like that.

The following are some examples of thinspiration slogans layered on top of images:

- "Nothing tastes as good as skinny feels."

- "Your body keeps an accurate journal, regardless of what you write down."

- "Sacrifice is giving up something good for something better."

- "To sit down and still have a flat stomach."

- "Because the fat won't melt itself."

- "You don't get what you want; you get what you work for."

- "To finally ask a store if they carry a size 0."

- "A moment on the lips, forever on the hips."

- "So that when you look at yourself in the mirror, you can smile."

- "Eat clean and stay lean."

Once a thinspiration image is created (and it could be made by *anyone*—from a student to a major advertising company), it is shared with the public on social media websites, such as Instagram, Facebook, Twitter, Pinterest, and Tumblr. It's all too easy for anyone to spread dangerous images and messages.

Websites that share thinspiration are commonly used by young women with eating disorders like anorexia and bulimia, who use the images as aids in their disorders; girls look at these pictures on the internet for motivation as they interact with each other online and encourage each other to diet.

This behavior is extremely harmful. The internet can be a great resource for receiving support from others, but it can also be dangerous because girls can meet people who are misinformed and preoccupied with being thin. Sometimes searching for and sharing thinspiration images lead young women to a specific online community of like-minded females that is even more dangerous: pro-ana and pro-mia.

"We need to promote that beautiful women come in many forms."

—SANY GUEST

Pro-ana and pro-mia organizations promote the eating disorders anorexia and bulimia. They claim that the behavior of these disorders is normal, despite the disturbing effects, and that these disorders represent a lifestyle choice rather than a mental illness. Without proper support systems or information, young women in these communities help each other engage in anorexia or bulimia, sharing tips for quick weight loss in a variety of dangerous ways, including overexercising, undereating, and binge eating. The conversations on these community websites range from thigh gaps, how to keep from eating food, diet pills, and laxatives to—of course—thinspiration.

Trigger Warning. Here is an example of a pro-ana Tumblr post by thintillyoubreak.

I hate this.

To eat is to die, and to starve is to live.

But starving is slowly killing yourself.

To be as light as air.

To be as a whiff of smoke, to move graceful and float and curl up around the others.

To become transparent and to disappear.

I will accept that air that is within me,

It is all I need to survive.

Drunk of water. Feeding on the air.

Reducing and disappearing until I am nothing,

but gone.

Another popular topic in the #thinspo community is thigh gaps. Getting and keeping a thigh gap is extremely desirable to people in the world of pro-ana and pro-mia websites. Having a thigh gap means that one's legs are so skinny that the insides of the thighs do not touch. Girls in these communities encourage each other to go to great lengths to try to achieve thigh gaps. Many feel it's something they should aspire to because they often notice it on models and celebrities in the media. Again, media images are what convince girls this extreme look is ideal, and yet again, girls may be unaware that Photoshop is commonly used on photos to create thigh gaps. They are misinformed that this look can be achieved by diet, exercise, or other pro-ana or pro-mia methods. In actuality, a girl's genetics determine the width of her hips, which in turn determines the distance between her legs and whether she will have a gap between them. Misinformation about thigh gaps is just one example of how wrong advice can influence many girls to go to dangerous lengths to achieve an unattainable look.

Since thinspiration is a fairly recent phenomenon, not a lot of information exists about what it is, what the long- or short-term effects of it are, or how to deal with it.

> Right now, other people's personal experiences about how to handle it are the best education for girls.

Victoria Gigante is a former model turned life coach who wrote about her experience working as an extremely thin model and about the negative costs associated with it. For example, at age twenty-six, she developed osteoporosis as a result of her anorexia. Gigante wants girls and young women to know that thin models may seem glamorous and beautiful, but there are a lot of hidden problems associated with maintaining that level of thinness. To her, thinspiration images confirm that society needs to become more informed about the problems that accompany undereating and overexercising.

I asked Adrienne Ressler of the Renfrew Center whether thinspiration images and websites play a part in creating body dissatisfaction or eating disorders. She stated two poignant facts:

1. Thinspiration websites provide a place and a voice where individuals can receive validation (positive reinforcement) for their disorder.

2. Those who are vulnerable to this type of validation (that is, very likely to be affected by it) can become dependent on it, which helps maintain their disorder.

It is unlikely that thinspiration images alone cause eating disorders; Ressler explained that some girls who view these images and websites will resist their message and know that they are unhealthy. Unfortunately, not all girls are able to do so. Ultimately, thinspiration is a negative support system that justifies dangerous thinking and behaviors.

> "You don't encourage people to take care of their body by telling them to hate it."
>
> —*Laci Green*

Those who share thinspiration images should educate themselves about this issue and devote more resources to banning those images. If social media websites were monitored more carefully, family, friends, doctors, and therapists could better fight the misinformation posted and find ways to offer support to girls in pro-ana and pro-mia communities.

Thinspiration and fitspiration images are not inspiring. They promote negative body images and the false idea that being healthy is equal to being thin. They pretend to motivate, but really they make women feel inadequate. Thinspiration will continue to surface and become more popular if we don't do something about it. In order to inspire girls to be happy with their average, beautiful body types, we need to establish images of healthier, more diverse women in the media.

"When women believe they are enough and realize their own potential, embrace their natural gifts, they are inherently beautiful."

—BRIANA BACHUS

Getting to Know You

Now it's time to ask yourself some questions and reflect on those answers. Fill in your responses in the provided spaces, or use a personal journal. Be open and honest with yourself. Don't be afraid to explore your thoughts, no matter how delicate or personal they may feel. This is the time for you to recognize your own beauty and learn about yourself.

If you found out that one of your friends was looking online for tips on anorexic or bulimic behavior, what would you say to her?

_____

_____

_____

_____

_____

_____

Write an inspiring message to yourself.

_____

_____

_____

_____

_____

_____

Chapter at a Glance

- Thinspiration and fitspiration use images of female bodies, along with slogans, to inspire viewers to try to achieve a thin body ideal.

- Thinspiration can be easily found on different social media platforms. This is a problem because anyone can create or view these images.

- Thinspiration promotes negative body images and the idea that thin equals healthy, *which is not true.*

- Pro-ana and pro-mia websites offer girls dangerous tips and encouragement for their anorexic or bulimic behavior.

- We need to monitor harmful misinformation about thinness and inspire girls to be happy with their average body types.

"I feel like beauty starts from the inside and then can be portrayed on the outside through different ways."

—CHEYENNE COUTO

Average Girls: Thoughts from *Real* Girls on Thinspiration

"I used to be impacted hugely by thinspiration. I had a diary where I would make thinspiration collages."

—*Rebecca*

"Thinspiration is daft. As long as you are . . . healthy . . . then you are perfect."

—*Kayleigh*

"Thinspiration is scary. I actually had an anonymous fitspiration account and was shocked at what I saw. Just as concerning is how many girls with eating disorders also are into various other forms of self-harm. So scary and so sad."

—*Michelle*

"I regularly compare myself to thinspiring people: people in the media, celebrities, etc. Then I remind myself to look at my biggest celebrity idols and notice that they aren't necessarily thin with perfect hair and makeup and amazing clothes. I idolize them for their talents, passions, skills, and the beauty I see radiating through. Sometimes they are also thin and perfect looking, and that is depressing."

—*Claira*

"I used negative pictures with comments to try to inspire myself to lose weight. My boyfriend ripped them all down though."

—*Karie*

"I think the media has a big influence on people. Without even realizing it, people connect advertisements, movies, songs, etc., to their personal lives and compare things in detail. Watching a Victoria's Secret commercial, I can't help but think how nice it would be to be as pretty as the models and have a body as nice as theirs.

"Although I would love to have a Victoria's Secret model's body, I wouldn't consider them my thinspiration because I know that it isn't realistic for me, and I'm only setting myself up for failure and never achieving that goal. I use Tumblr for fitspiration and try to avoid thinspiration because thinspiration is mostly negative and about girls throwing up or starving themselves.

"Also, I find myself constantly comparing myself to other girls at school, and even people walking down the street. It always seems that I can pick out the good in others but never the good in myself."

—*Amanda*

"The internet has provided the perfect platform for thinspiration and for the reinforcement of eating disorders. Unfortunately, young women and older women alike can find self-harming information through Facebook, Pinterest, Twitter, etc. And somehow, in most of the online world, thinspiration has become normal and acceptable. Those who fight against this mainstream acceptance of this portrayal of our bodies haven't been able to be loud enough to cancel out the negativity and destructiveness of these sites and ways of thinking."

—*Kat*

"I think thinspiration should be banned and set on fire. The media also needs to cut the Photoshop crap and accept that no asses were created equal and that no woman can be 5 foot 11 and ninety pounds *with* curves."

—*Laura*

"Thinspiration is stupid. You should strive to be healthy, and I think that's something girls should know themselves. Social media like Tumblr, where 99 percent of the pictures of people are of girls who fit society's ridiculous standards of beauty, spurs on all this bad stuff."

—*Alexa*

"I think thinspiration is disgusting. It pains me to even write the word! I wish there were more campaigns like the Dove Campaign for Real Beauty. . . . With eating disorders having the highest mortality rate of any mental illness, more money and education need to be spent on the community and health professionals."

—*Sherry*

"The ultra-thinness of models is not attainable by most women without severe health consequences."

—*Tammy*

"I've always compared myself to images in the media and thinspiration because they always make it sound like that's how you have to be to feel good about yourself and be considered beautiful to everyone else. I've learned that the media is putting us down about cellulite and fat and other normal things."

—*Heidi*

"'Thinspiration' is a disgusting term. The media needs to present realistic body images."

—*Tina*

> "I've heard people say that thinspiration is just a way to motivate girls to drop down to a healthy weight and maintain that weight. But there's nothing healthy about being too thin. Some girls are naturally thin, which is fine, but maintaining a healthy weight for your body type and height doesn't always mean being pin thin."
>
> —*Emily*

"I think we live in a society with a hyperawareness of obesity and eating disorders, but we're simultaneously unwilling to teach people, especially girls, how to be healthy. We'll sit around pointing blame at video games or at whatever the target of the week happens to be, but nobody will say what needs to be said.

"I'm not saying we should tell girls to be ashamed of their bodies, but if we're going to be honest, then 'healthy is beautiful' needs to be the message! I get freedom of speech and all that jazz, but thinspiration scares me to death. It's an entire community of girls who are encouraging each other to starve themselves to death. Congratulations, society: You've fallen off the deep end!

"I see girls on forum-style websites . . . who act like bulimia or anorexia nervosa are just diets, not life-threatening illnesses. I responded to a girl the other day who wanted to know how to use laxatives as a weight-loss tool. It's genuinely terrifying to see the rampant lack of education or the blatant misinformation being perpetuated, or kept going, by other girls, schools, and even parents. Something somewhere has *got* to change.

". . . The media is ruthless and, more importantly, careless. Every time a celebrity gets pregnant, there are articles for weeks on end about how they're super fat and how they need to stop eating so much. *Hello, gaining weight is basically your only job when you're pregnant!* Granted, there's healthy and unhealthy, but that's their business. It shouldn't be up to the paparazzi to make these women feel awful about themselves."

—*Chelsea*

"People will relate more to women with normal flaws."

—*Chantel*

"Social media can be motivating and toxic. You have to be able to police yourself from getting sucked into unrealistic wants or comparisons. I try to find pictures I think are beautiful, analyze why they're beautiful, and then apply the why to myself. Thinness doesn't equal beauty."

—*Alanna*

"There's very little I can say to anybody who is young right now who wants to grow up to be beautiful, except: Don't make beauty your goal. It will only put you in a spiral. Make your goal being kind, or having a good job, or traveling the world."

—*Genni*

"I hate the saying, 'Nothing tastes as good as skinny feels.' I used to think I would never be happy if I wasn't skinny, because I saw all the skinny models and actresses in magazines, but I wasted too much time on that and wound up harming myself. Be yourself. I'm fat and I'm attractive. Period."

—*Cupcake*

Chapter 6
MENTAL HEALTH

· ·

Without positive media, it is nearly impossible for us to combat the many mental and physical health issues that women face as a result of negative body image, including depression. *Depression* is a serious medical condition with a variety of symptoms, including extreme sadness. A depressed person often feels hopeless and has no energy or interest in life. Depression is caused not by one single factor but by a combination of factors, such as biology, genetics, gender, age, trauma, stress, medication, and many others.

Society's body image ideals can be a major factor in causing depression in females, especially those who have eating disorders. Young women experience more self-consciousness and judgment than boys do. As young women develop, they are three times more likely than boys to suffer from depression. Experiences with negative body image contribute to the development of depression. In fact, girls aged ten to fourteen are five times more likely than boys to be hospitalized for attempted suicide.

> Suicidal thoughts in girls of this age are often linked to negative body image and low self-esteem.

There is also a high rate of suicide in girls who suffer from anorexia and bulimia; it is a major cause of death among patients with an eating disorder. As a girl's body dissatisfaction increases and as eating disorders develop, the symptoms of depression often become worse. In fact, "nearly 50 percent of people with eating disorders also meet the criteria for depression."

An *eating disorder* is a serious mental illness that involves major disturbances in one's eating behavior. Eating disorders are one of the most damaging mental illnesses girls can suffer from. According to the National Eating Disorders Association, eating disorders can develop and return at any age; however, there is shocking confirmation that they can start as early as five or six.

> Like depression, eating disorders are not linked to one single factor; they are often caused by many factors, including psychological problems, genetics, gender, family and personal relationships, social pressure, and low self-esteem.

Social ideologies centered upon the importance of thinness can act as a trigger for initial weight loss attempts. When combined with other factors (like genetics), an eating disorder can emerge and be maintained as a result of additional factors (such as environment).

Eating disorders have incredibly devastating effects. Some of the possible effects of an eating disorder include hair loss, osteoporosis, dehydration, bowel paralysis, and cardiac arrest. Anorexia nervosa has the "highest mortality rate of any psychiatric illness." This means that anorexia causes more people to die than any other mental illness. "It is estimated that 10% of individuals with AN [anorexia nervosa] will die within 10 years of the onset of the disorder."

Many women attempt to lose weight by restricting their food intake and exercising; those with eating disorders may do the same but excessively. They also attempt to control their weight with more extreme methods. Often eating disorders develop when a person focuses too much on controlling her weight or thinness. She might also fixate on a particular part of her body that dissatisfies her and turn to controlling her weight as a way of feeling "better." For example, to her, "it seems . . . easier to do something about body weight than overly narrow shoulders, short legs, or being broad-hipped." Adrienne Ressler of the Renfrew Center explained to me that girls with eating disorders are obsessed with their bodies and, essentially, live in their heads because they are so disconnected from their bodies.

Many people believe that eating disorders go hand in hand with anxiety disorders. *Anxiety*, or fear and nervousness, is a normal reaction to stress. However, the amount of anxiety a person experiences is determined by many factors, including genetics,

"I like that my body is different from others. Whether it's my colorful tattoos or the numerous scars from past surgeries, my body tells an adventurous story."

—CLAIRE BUCHANAN

psychology, and environment. When feelings of anxiety start to interfere with daily life, an anxiety disorder develops. There are several different types of anxiety disorders, but all of them cause extreme feelings of irrational fear and dread.

> Women, from puberty to age fifty, are nearly twice as likely as men to develop an anxiety disorder.

Often people have anxiety disorders before they develop eating disorders, and even if they start to recover from the eating disorder, they can still have the anxiety disorder.

It is important to know about the many different kinds of eating disorders that exist for women so that we can offer support to those affected by them and support ourselves as well. Without treatment, eating disorders will only get worse. They can be treated with different forms of therapy and sometimes by medication. If you or somebody you know is experiencing one of these illnesses, please talk to a doctor!

Types of Eating Disorders

- ANOREXIA NERVOSA sufferers have an intense fear of becoming fat or gaining weight, even when they are underweight. They starve themselves of food, refusing to maintain a normal body weight for their age and height. Someone with anorexia has a body weight less than 85 percent of the average and denies just how serious her current low body weight is. She may have an abnormal menstrual cycle or no menstruation at all. Anorexia can cause "serious health problems including bone loss, shrinking of vital organs and heart problems, which can lead to death."
  Atypical anorexia is another facet of this disorder. It is diagnosed when a person meets all of the criteria for anorexia nervosa, "except that despite significant weight loss, the individual's weight is within or above the normal range." An atypical anorexic meets anorexia criteria except for their weight (although they can still be in a state of malnourishment).

- BULIMIA NERVOSA sufferers have episodes of binge eating (eating large amounts of food in one sitting), followed by purging (trying to get rid of the food they've eaten so they won't gain weight). They use unhealthy methods to purge, like making themselves vomit, using laxatives, fasting, or exercising excessively. Someone with bulimia binge eats to gain a sense of escape from thoughts and feelings; she has a lack of control while eating. However, after the bingeing, she feels guilt and shame and then depression and anxiety about her behavior. These feelings create a self-perpetuating cycle.

Physical side effects of bulimia nervosa include tooth decay (from stomach acid eroding the tooth enamel), ulcers, gastro issues, and electrolyte imbalances that can affect major organs (like causing heart or kidney failure).

- BODY DYSMORPHIC DISORDER sufferers are overly focused on some flaw (real or imagined) on the body. This disorder is "similar to eating disorders in that both involve a concern with body image. However, a person with an eating disorder worries about weight and the shape of the entire body, while a person with BDD is concerned about a specific body part." A person with this disorder might start doing repetitive behaviors like looking in a mirror, picking at her skin, or trying to hide the supposed flaw. People with body dysmorphic disorder are often concerned with the size of their breasts or thighs, their hair, their facial features, or imperfections in their skin.

- BINGE EATING DISORDER sufferers eat large amounts of food in a short period of time while feeling like they can't stop themselves from eating. Unlike bulimia, no purging is involved in this disorder. Someone with binge eating disorder often eats alone and in secret because of guilt, embarrassment, and distress about her behavior. She overeats in an attempt to comfort herself and to avoid uncomfortable situations or feelings.

- ANOREXIA ATHLETICA, or sports anorexia, sufferers are compelled to exercise excessively. This means that they feel an irresistible urge to exercise in order to feel in control and to gain a sense of power and self-respect. Someone with anorexia athletica is obsessed with her weight and diet. She takes on challenging exercises and is never satisfied with her physical achievements. She will also insist that constantly exercising equals being healthy.

- ORTHOREXIA sufferers are obsessive about eating healthy. Their fixation on healthy eating can lead to nutritional deficiencies and illness.

With eating disorders, the key to recovery is intervention, with early intervention in the development of the disorder being most effective. The Renfrew Center is a treatment facility for people with eating disorders. They believe that the best way to aid their clients is to help them reconnect with their bodies. Adrienne Ressler explained to me that this disconnection happens when a person doesn't access the senses, emotions, and experiences stored in her body. The goal of the program is to teach young women to access their feelings so they can begin to heal. Healing is encouraged through many different types of therapies, including art therapy and dance movement, which help girls truly experience their bodies.

> **Many girls will never develop a full-blown eating disorder, yet they still might invest much of their energy and time in dealing with the societal pressure to achieve an ideal body.**

By age seventeen, 89 percent of girls have dieted, and "over one-half of teenage girls . . . use unhealthy weight control behaviors such as skipping meals, fasting, [or] smoking cigarettes." All the time they spend engulfed in this type of thinking and behavior can lead girls to blame themselves for failing to achieve unattainable standards.

> While we cannot completely blame the media for causing eating disorders, we do need to acknowledge the large role it plays.

We can stop spreading the negativity that reinforces eating disorders by discovering what information about them is available and by learning to decipher which information and images are truthful and which are damaging.

Social media websites provide great places for us to discuss our feelings and seek out support, but few are monitored for harmful content, so there is no guarantee that the information shared on these platforms is correct. Because so much false information exists on the internet, the National Health Education Standards were developed for youth "to increase their health literacy—their ability to find, understand, and use information and services to enhance health." It is extremely important to develop the critical skills necessary to seek out and understand correct information. Far too many internet sources provide false information that promotes the idea that thinness equals health.

"We are
all unique."

—SARAH DIONYSUS

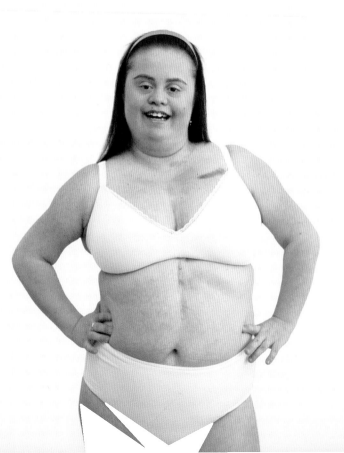

"What makes us different is what makes us all beautiful."

—FRANCIE MUNOZ

We need society to encourage healthy lifestyles that include healthy eating (not too much or too little) and being active within our ability. We need to shift focus from being thin and sexy to being healthy and confident, regardless of size. We need to learn and then teach others how to be critical of the media's obsession with thinness and understand that making negative statements about other people's bodies is a form of harassment.

Getting to Know You

Now it's time to ask yourself some questions and reflect on those answers. Fill in your responses in the provided spaces, or use a personal journal. Be open and honest with yourself. Don't be afraid to explore your thoughts, no matter how delicate or personal they may feel. This is the time for you to recognize your own beauty and learn about yourself.

How do you make yourself feel better when you feel sad?

Have you ever engaged in any of the following disordered eating behaviors?

- Making an excuse for not eating.

- Preferring to eat alone.

- Eating an unreasonably large amount of food.

- Making yourself vomit after eating.

- Obsessing over counting the calories you eat.

- Going a long period of time without eating.

- Using laxatives or diuretics (also called "water pills") to control your weight.

- Hiding your eating habits from others.

_____

_____

_____

_____

_____

Do you have any fears or anxiety about gaining weight or becoming fat? How can you combat those fears?

_____

_____

_____

_____

_____

"We are all
different and
that is good."

—HAILEY DOBBINS

Chapter at a Glance

- *Depression* is a medical condition that causes people to feel extreme sadness and lack of energy or interest in life.

- An *eating disorder* is a serious mental illness that involves major disturbances in eating behaviors. It is related to anxiety and fear of losing control.

- *Anxiety* is a normal reaction to stress. When you have excessive feelings of fear or dread, anxiety may interfere with your daily life.

- Mental illnesses (such as depression, eating disorders, and anxiety disorders) can overlap and affect each other's development. They are all caused by a variety of factors.

- There are several different types of eating disorders, including anorexia nervosa, bulimia nervosa, body dysmorphic disorder, binge eating disorder, anorexia athletica, and orthorexia.

- Many girls dabble in disordered eating, though their experiences do not necessarily lead to a full-blown eating disorder.

- Intervention is key to recovery. Many support systems are available.

Average Girls: Thoughts from *Real* Girls on Mental Health

"I have dealt with depression for the majority of my life. I've had an eating disorder for over a decade and like it. I will never stop."

—*Ashton*

"To sum it up in the most simplistic way, I was literally dying from anorexia. For over a decade, I was trapped inside my head, experiencing eating disorder behaviors across a wide spectrum—from bingeing on massive quantities of food and purging it all afterward, to fasting for days on end without putting anything in my body. I was, to say the least, a complete mess.

"The actual behaviors were minimal in comparison to the terrible thought processes that constantly streamed through my mind. My eating disorder had managed throughout the years to create in me core beliefs about myself that were the most horrid descriptive words that could ever be used to describe anything. Every day, I would awaken from my restless night and battle getting out of bed, wondering why I was alive. Questioning what purpose I had because no one loved me, and I deserved absolutely nothing."

—*Kelly*

"Dieting works but is hard to stick to. I wish I had the willpower to have an eating disorder. I don't feel depressed at all. I tried one diet where I lost eleven pounds in a week through eating around 300 calories a day and working off anything over that on a cross-trainer."

—*Tamara*

"I suffer from depression and have struggled with my weight since about sixth grade. I am very uncomfortable in my body. I have tried everything possible to lose weight and eat healthy."

—Kayla

"A few years ago, I managed to get down to 135 [pounds], but it wasn't good enough. I started dating a guy and put on weight, then suffered from severe depression and was put on medication. My weight ballooned up. I tried Weight Watchers, starvation, diet pills, laxatives, Herbal Magic, and even bought thyroid pills as well.

"When I got off my depression meds, I gained an additional twenty pounds. I'm struggling to lose it and, as a result, have been speaking to a dietician who won't help me until I have a breakthrough with my counselor. She says I have an eating disorder, but unfortunately, no weight loss."

—Karie

"My mother often criticized me for being 'too fat' or told me to watch what I eat because she said I'd grow up to look like her. I was anorexic from the ages of thirteen to twenty-two."

—Rachel

"I am an emotional overeater. It sucks. It's something that comes and goes. But it's been a struggle for me for as long as I can remember. I eat when I'm happy, or bored, or sad, or frustrated. I eat when I'm full, because if I don't eat that handful of pretzels, my mind can't shut off until I do. I'm making an effort to change that habit, but it's hard. My biggest fear is passing that on to my daughter."

—Erin

"I'm nineteen and have been struggling with depression, anorexia, and cutting since seventh grade."

—*Alli*

"I moved when I was in the ninth grade, and in tenth grade my parents announced that they were getting a divorce. From that point, things turned chaotic. The thoughts in my head were spiraling and everything felt totally out of control.

"At that point, my eating disorder came to my rescue. Or so I thought. It falsely gave me something I felt I could control, and it assisted with my anxiety over change. Over the years, my eating disorder became my identity. I got to a point where my disordered thoughts and behaviors controlled almost everything that I did."

—*Kelly*

"I'm a thin girl and always have been. I've never had an eating disorder or any issues with food, but have always been called anorexic or too skinny. I've had friends pull at my skin and tell me I should eat more. I've had people tell me I should eat a meal or a burger and try to force food on me."

—*Leesha*

"I was pretty close to having an eating disorder. I used to eat nothing until dinner and had a maximum of 300 calories a day, which would all be at dinner. Then a guy friend told me that boys like bums and boobs and that he'd always found me attractive. He had a girlfriend, but his words have stuck."

—*Tanya*

"I struggle with depression. I often can't tell if I'm depressed from my negative body image or if I have a negative body image because I'm depressed. I often try to eat healthy and stick to an exercise routine. I often think about dieting, but logic myself out of it."

—*Alanna*

"One way in which my boyfriend is not perfect is his preference for very thin women. It hasn't been a problem [for] a few years, but I used to see him ogling and it made me absolutely terrified. I was so scared he was going to leave me because I wasn't thin. That was my most disordered period. I kept losing weight, and I wanted him to feel guilty about it.

"I don't blame the media for eating disorders one bit. I think that you really have to already hate yourself to develop an eating disorder. Girls with eating disorders have pasts full of abuse, or are Type A personalities who are never satisfied with themselves."

—*Chantel*

"I don't have any clinical disorders, but I think all women probably show signs of some symptoms, or at least of the language and the thoughts around eating, dieting, exercise, etc."

—*Louise*

"I've had an eating disorder for three years. I purged everything I ate. At first, I would only purge if I'd had something unhealthy or 'bad,' but then I started to do it with everything I ate. I saw a therapist and I'm fine now. But eating disorder thoughts are starting to slowly creep back. My mom is a huge health nut and exercise freak, so that doesn't really help."

—*Kate*

"I started to go out less at night after [my dance] shows, got up early to go to the gym, and went out . . . with my friends less often. I started to control my diet. Watermelon and fiber cereal for breakfast and before shows as a snack. Salads the rest of the time. Then I added a second gym session at night, before dinner, even if it was before the show we did at night. I didn't look very well. My costumes were too big and my energy level was low. My co-dancers even started to hang out with me less. I wasn't a happy person to be around and I never wanted to have fun. I was a hassle when we went out for meals. I was always ordering weird things or eating nothing at all.

"I kept doing what I was doing until the dance captain put me on an official weight warning. I was proud of myself, and for once I felt pretty. Why is it that feeling pretty, a positive feeling, can come from such a negative thing as thinness? I hated it, but liked it. I had my 'wall' up. Nothing could help me. I had counseling. I liked going because . . . now I had the attention of everyone.

"I started to research what other girls were eating and restricting and how they lessened their caloric intake. One girl ate only red Skittles on Mondays. Tuesdays were for yellow, and so on. Only one pack of Skittles a week. One girl was a condiment eater, like I was. I snuck snacks at night when no one was watching. It took me *hours* to shop at the supermarket, as I would look at calorie counts, ingredients, and other such information, and shop for the smallest amounts of everything. I even recall going to a baseball game with my brother, buying him a hotdog, and then, when he wasn't watching, I filled a cup with relish and ate that (a condiment) for lunch.

"After gaining weight, I lost the feeling of a lack of control that I once had. In the end, the nutritionists and psychologists classified me as having sports anorexia."

—*Melissa*

"I have been living with depression for almost nine years now. I went on several diets in high school and was obsessed with how many calories I ate. I have never been skinny, and I often get upset because it doesn't seem fair to me."

—Stephanie

"Dieting is not something I firmly believe in. As for myself, in order to maintain my body weight, I count calories. Eating disorders are common among kids my age, but they aren't talked about. Due to the pressure to be thin, I often try to purge after eating. I'm not always successful, but either way, I still feel terrible about myself afterward.

"Although I've never been diagnosed with depression, I do often find myself feeling sad most of the time. I don't have thoughts of suicide, but I have cut myself before, due to being unhappy. I think that depression is becoming more and more common as more people become aware of it. Before, it was never really talked about, but now it has been exposed."

—Amanda

"I think there's a misconception that eating disorders affect only girls. . . . As for depression, I think having a bad self-image can affect your mental health drastically."

—Jess

"I am bipolar. Without my meds, I am a disaster and hate myself and self-mutilate. With my meds, I am a completely different person. I no longer diet; I simply eat very healthy."

—Wendy

"When I was in seventh grade, I was 'involved' with this guy (about as involved as two twelve-year-olds can be). His previous girlfriends were both petite, thin girls, and I just wasn't. I was taller and curvy— not overweight or anything, but I wasn't petite.

"When things started going south with this guy, I thought it was because I wasn't like his last girlfriends. I started trying to lose weight by exercising all the time, but it didn't do anything. So I stopped eating breakfast, and that soon became skipping lunch as well. I had a small snack if I felt sick, but other than that, I just ate dinner because my mom forced me to. I started losing weight, but the more people told me I looked great, the more I thought I must have looked awful before. I started having issues with my friends, which just perpetuated the negative feelings.

"This went on for about ten months. I don't remember how much weight I lost. It never became a critical thing, but it was a really dark time. It came back in tenth grade, and that was an incredibly dark year as well. I was very depressed and my habit of skipping meals came back. It was like a switch went off, and I could feel it happening, but I couldn't figure out how to stop it. All I knew was that everything was out of control and nobody else seemed to notice. The only people who did were the guys who wanted to take advantage of it, which made it that much worse."

—Chelsea

"I suffer from depression and anxiety. It isn't caused by self-image distortion, but can definitely be fueled by it."

—Claira

"I have depression, I'm currently on a diet, and I have an eating disorder."

—Kay

"Dieting isn't bad to a point, if you just want to be healthier. Eating disorders are hard to deal with, but there is always help. I myself have depression and always have, but with the right help (meds, therapy, hobbies, friends and family, etc.), it is bearable and doesn't ruin your life."

—Arielle

"I've had minor problems with dieting, but I am lucky to be surrounded now by positivity. I know my friends have suffered from disordered eating. I am lucky to be able to support them. It's very widespread and nearly every teen at school knows somebody who has an eating problem. It needs addressing."

—Rebecca

"I see eating as mechanical, a thing I have to do to live. Hence, I don't like doing it."

—Leonie

"I have always had an eating disorder. I was always called chubby by my mother. I was always compared to my cousins, and I wasn't able to go to dance classes because I was too chubby . . . so I developed bulimia. It was easy to hide; mints, mouthwash, etc., helped mask the bad breath. Then I discovered exercise, so my diet then became exercise. Then I discovered yoga, meditation, and Buddhism, and I am learning to love the curves that I was gifted with."

—Lina

"I also believe that nothing makes you feel better about yourself than when you are able to make someone else feel good about themselves."

—HEATHER CLIFFORD

"It all started with trying to lose weight so I could finally 'fit in and look good' for high school. But I found that I just couldn't stop losing weight because I never felt skinny enough, even when I was underweight. I'm now about eight months into recovery and doing so much better, and I really want to reach out and help other people too. I also know about six other friends who have an eating disorder or multiple eating disorders.

"I've happily gained some weight since I became underweight, and I'm learning to love myself exactly as I am."

—Heidi

"I suffered from an eating disorder for fifteen years and went to treatment to save my life. I am currently in recovery and will stay in recovery. I have a new sense of life, and life is so much clearer when you are feeding your brain."

—Sherry

"I think if you're dieting, you should do it safely. There should be enough education in school that girls know never to starve themselves, or throw up their food on purpose, or cut themselves because they hate their bodies, because it just makes things bad. But there is no education, not even a little.

"Magazines and fashion shows should stop showing little stick women who obviously barely eat, because that perpetuates all of the illnesses girls develop. But they will not do that because they don't care. Someone should be telling girls that society's standards are dumb and ridiculous."

—Alexa

"I grew up as a ballet dancer and struggled with anorexia from ages twelve to seventeen, then spent two years in intensive outpatient treatment. I quit ballet in the course of my recovery in an effort to form a new identity, find my voice, and learn who I really was.

"My recovery led me to college, and the pursuit of college scholarships led me to compete in the Miss America Pageant at the local level. I was shocked when I won Miss Oakland County, and even more shocked when I won Miss Michigan, and then Miss America just a year after I'd entered my first pageant. It was terrifying and exciting, but mostly, the experience helped me find my voice.

"I had chosen as my platform eating disorders awareness and education. I had the incredible opportunity to travel 20,000 miles a month and talk to young women on a daily basis about rejecting the cultural stereotype of beauty. Thankfully, they listened to me because I was so close to their age and was also in the entertainment world. I could tell them firsthand that [the] world was not as perfect and glamorous as it seemed.

"From my own struggle and recovery, I learned that as women, we all struggle hugely, emotionally, and deeply—not only so that we can grow and learn to become stronger, but also so that we can reach out and help others."

—*Kirsten Haglund, Miss America 2008*

Chapter 7
BULLYING AND
SEXUAL HARASSMENT

· ·

We constantly compare ourselves to others because of societal ideologies we've subconsciously picked up. Society teaches us, as women, to judge those who don't fit into ideal standards. Boys also learn to judge females by their appearance and how well they meet society's beauty standards. Girls with low self-esteem experience significant body dissatisfaction because they are more vulnerable to social pressure about body ideals.

> When a girl is hard on herself, she faces her own inner
> bully. As a result, she may become a bully to others.

Bullying is the act of frightening, threatening, or hurting other people. Bullies often act this way because they are trying to feel better about their own poor self-esteem; they transfer their own feelings of unworthiness onto the person they are bullying.

> Young people who have poor body image are more likely to
> either bully others or be the target of bullying.

Bullying is an ongoing problem. About one in three students in Canada have reported being bullied, and nearly half of Canadian parents report that their child has been a bullying victim.

"We need to show
[girls] that we are
all exquisitely
beautiful—
naturally."

—SARAH LEACH

Girls who bully often engage in a kind of bullying called *relational aggression*. A bully who shows relational aggression does not physically injure her victim but instead harms her by damaging her relationships and social status (how other people think of her). Relational aggression can involve name-calling, criticizing the victim's appearance, spreading rumors about her, and excluding her from groups or activities (from not inviting her to a party to refusing to be her partner for a school project).

> **Many bullies will focus on making fun of her target's body image or size. This behavior is not surprising when this type of bullying is essentially approved by our society.**

Look at the level of importance our culture places on the way people—especially females—look. Girls who are slightly overweight are more likely to be teased, and teasing can naturally cause them to experience more body dissatisfaction than girls who do not get teased.

Girls often become bullies because they are jealous of something their target has or is. They also bully to feel like they have power over someone who appears weaker than them. At the time when girls' bodies are changing and developing due to puberty, a girl can be targeted by bullies just because of physical differences between her and the rest of her class (for example, because she experiences puberty earlier or later than her peers do). Being bullied can lead to negative body image, low self-esteem, eating disorders, and depression.

These days, young women face a form of bullying known as *cyberbullying*, or online harassment. This type of bullying is done through social media, websites, email, and texting, and it is yet another way that people spread harmful societal ideologies.

> **Cyberbullying can involve insulting and making fun of a person on social media or other websites, sharing her private images and messages with other people, and sending hurtful or threatening comments directly to her.**

Over the internet and phone networks, we can message, chat, text, and blog instantaneously. The downside is that we have little control over what happens to our images and texts once they're shared, and it's incredibly easy for such materials to spread to countless other people, including people you don't even know personally. Anyone can say anything about someone with little to no consequences.

Another problem with online communication is that it's easier to type something mean about a person than to say it to them in person. With traditional in-person bullying, the bullies may experience some compassion for the victim because they are face-to-face—in cyberbullying, there is little chance of this.

Another type of bullying is sexual harassment, which occurs both in person and over the internet.

Sexual harassment is "uninvited and unwelcome verbal or physical behavior of a sexual nature." A sexual harasser aims to embarrass, humiliate, and control another person based on their gender or sexual orientation. Many sexual harassers are heterosexual males. Sexual harassment is a means for them to establish their maleness. Witnessing it is one of the ways boys learn how to demonstrate societal ideologies. The media teaches boys that their role is to be the viewers of girls, who are objects. In other words, we are all living our lives through the lens of the male gaze and a culture of male dominance.

Sexual harassment has become a regular part of the school experience for females, and it often extends into other areas of their lives. It is often seen as normal to make sexual jokes to a female, touch her inappropriately, or comment on her physical appearance, and many dismiss this behavior as positive attention. Women are taught that being sexy makes them powerful. This is an illusion.

Girls who seek approval for the way they look are especially vulnerable to the constant media messages telling women they need to be sexy and beautiful for men. In fact, 27 percent of high school girls in Ontario, Canada, report that they have been pressured into doing something sexual they did not want to do. For example, Amanda Todd, a fifteen-year-old girl from British Columbia, Canada, was the victim of cyberbullying and harassment and committed suicide in 2012. Amanda's struggles began in seventh grade when an unknown man she was talking to via webcam convinced her to expose her breasts. Over the next few

"Some people won't be happy until they've pushed you to the ground. What you have to do is have the courage to stand your ground and not give them the time of day. Hold on to your power and never give it away."

—*Donna Schoenrock*

years, the man harassed Amanda online and shared her topless photo with her classmates and the general public to humiliate her. Tragically, instead of rallying around Amanda in support, her peers bullied and tormented her. She suffered severe depression and engaged in self-destructive behaviors before eventually committing suicide.

Many young girls like Amanda feel pressured into trying to be the type of girl the media encourages them to be, and as a result, they become targets of bullying. In Ontario, Canada, 46 percent of high school girls reported that they had been "the target of unwanted sexual comments or gestures." The effects of sexual harassment are far-reaching and often lead to the development of eating disorders, low self-esteem, and depression. Amanda Todd's case is just one example of how destructive and cruel bullying can be. We need to teach both girls and boys to accept each other's differences and to respect others' bodies.

Ideologies of thinness and beauty are reinforced not only by self-comparing but also by acting judgmental toward others. In the same way we develop negative body image through self-comparison, we spread similar seeds by judging others the way we've learned to judge ourselves—harshly. If we can fully understand the fact that we have internalized incorrect body image ideologies, why the media encourages them, and how society perpetuates them, then we can begin to challenge and deconstruct those ideologies.

IF SOMEONE IS BULLYING YOU,

- Know that it is wrong and do not allow others to convince you it is a minor issue.

- Ignore bullies by walking away. (Most bullies are looking for a reaction.)

- Tell someone you trust (*especially* an adult if you're a minor) about what happened.

- Be confident and hold your head up high.

- Do not fight back.

- Talk about how bullying makes you feel. (Talking will make you feel better and help you cope if you are bullied again.)

- Know that it is wrong and is not your fault. It does not matter whether you were being flirtatious or have been intimate in the past, whether you were under the influence of drugs or alcohol, or even whether you were dressed provocatively. Do not allow others to convince you harassment is a minor issue.

- Keep a record. Make detailed notes about when and where it occurred and what happened.

- If it is safe to do so, ask the harasser to stop. (For example, you can say, "It makes me uncomfortable when you do 'insert behavior.' Please stop or I will report you.")

- Tell someone you trust (*especially* an adult if you're a minor) about what happened. Speaking with a mental health professional (like a social worker or psychologist) can help too.

- Address it. If you are in school, you can report this type of behavior to a teacher or the school administration. If you are at work, you can talk to your supervisor, human resources manager, or union representative.

- Call the police. There are some situations where sexual harassment is against the law, such as threats, physical harm, stalking, or sexual behavior toward a minor.

Getting to Know You

Now it's time to ask yourself some questions and reflect on those answers. Fill in your responses in the provided spaces, or use a personal journal. Be open and honest with yourself. Don't be afraid to explore your thoughts, no matter how delicate or personal they may feel. This is the time for you to recognize your own beauty and learn about yourself.

Has anyone, including yourself, ever made a negative comment about your body? How did this make you feel? How did you respond?

_____

_____

_____

_____

_____

Have you ever made a hurtful comment to someone else? How did this make you feel? How do you think the other person felt?

_____

_____

_____

_____

_____

_____

Chapter at a Glance

- *Bullying* is the act of frightening, threatening, or hurting other people.

- Those who have a poor body image are more likely to be a bully or be bullied.

- *Relational aggression* is the most common form of bullying girls engage in; they hurt their victims in a social way, such as excluding them or gossiping about them.

- Bullying causes negative body image and low self-esteem and can lead to eating disorders and depression.

- *Cyberbullying* is especially harmful because bullies can easily hurt their targets without having to face them in person.

- *Sexual harassment* is unwanted verbal or physical behavior that is sexual in nature.

- Bullying has become a normal part of our day-to-day lives and reinforces societal ideologies.

- If you are being bullied, make sure you tell someone trustworthy!

- If you are being sexually harassed, remember that it is not your fault (regardless of what you were wearing or how you were acting). Keep a record and tell someone!

"Be proud of your curves, scars, and wrinkles; those are memories."

—KRYSTAL FRENCH

Average Girls: Thoughts from *Real* Girls on Bullying and Sexual Harassment

"I've had to deal with sexual harassment since I was in the fourth grade. It's very damaging to have been objectified from a young age."

—*Arielle*

"I've been bullied from the age of three for having a protruding stomach."

—*Laura*

"I used to be overweight, and I have been bullied about it. . . . It's wrong to make fun of someone for their weight. Sexual harassment shouldn't be such a common thing. Some women, however, may take it as a compliment and be flattered."

—*Pearl*

"I think the rise in technology's use and accessibility has led to an increase in bullying. As someone who was bullied throughout my childhood and into my teens, I know that bullying greatly contributes to your definition of yourself. This is a critical time of being assessed by your peers; your peer's opinions are very important in this period. I also think it is quite hard to shake these thoughts once you reach adulthood."

—*Nicole*

"I have received unwanted sexual attention due to my large bust size since I was twelve."

—*Michelle*

"After I was taken advantage of when I was under the influence of alcohol at a party over the weekend, the people at my school weren't so nice when they heard about the things that happened to me. The guy who had been with me told everyone at school and people mocked me for months. He didn't really have to tell people; the large hickey on my neck was enough evidence that something had happened. The rumors eventually traveled to other schools and I had people confront me about it.

"Now, everyone at school ignores me. I feel like I am alone and no one likes me. People call me names, shut me down when I try to speak to them, and people who used to be my friends won't even talk to me. One girl who I'd considered my best friend won't even stick up for me. I am shunned by the people who used to be my friends. I'm known as a slut and I've had many guys come up to me asking for 'favors.'

"The way people have treated me makes me feel really bad about myself. I honestly believe that if I were prettier or thinner, people would be able to tolerate me more and I wouldn't be in this situation."

—Amanda

"I was sexually harassed and bullied by more people than I can count. Rape culture and sexualization and gender culture need to end if we are to fix body image. The two are wound together tightly in an ugly rope that victims/survivors end up hanging themselves with."

—Leonie

"I was bullied all through my childhood, and yes, I was sexually harassed as a young teen. It distorts everything you think you know. Even if you know better, you think, 'What if they're right? What if I really am worthless and nobody would miss me?' It messes with your head, that's for sure."

—Jenni

"I've experienced sexual harassment since the sixth grade. My breast development was much faster than most girls. I think I was probably a C in my freshman year of high school, and at twenty, I'm now a G. What kills me is that it started with the girls! I'd hear girls spreading rumors that I was a slut, whore, etc., because of my breast size. Guys would stare at my chest all the time. I distinctly remember the catty popular girls saying I was a slut because I wore shirts that showed cleavage. I was so upset! When you have large breasts, that's about the only kind of shirt out there. It wasn't like they were falling out of my shirt or anything like that.

"When people see a well-endowed girl, they make immediate assumptions about the kind of person she is. Thinking back, I've gotten more sexual harassment from other girls than I have from guys. I don't get it."

—*Chelsea*

"Being fat gets you lots of bullying, even at an older age. And sexual harassment is everywhere. People single you out, and if you are different from them, you are the victim of their pent-up aggression."

—*Tammy*

"I think women learn from a young age to put up with bullying and sexual harassment. Most women never feel safe. As children and as young adults, they are often bullied by fellow females—ostracized, teased for being 'too feminine' or not feminine enough, etc.—and are sexually harassed by males about breast size, puberty, sexual activity, or lack thereof.

"With no escape, women learn to accept negative comments and harassment for their entire lives, and many internalize these comments. Bullying and sexual harassment feed the depression and eating disorders and can continue to do so into adulthood for many women."

—*Kat*

"As a child I was sexually abused. I swore I wouldn't have sex until I was married, and I never planned on getting married. The fact that I was twenty, fat, and a virgin made me the butt of quite a number of jokes, and this was from so-called friends. I think because I lacked confidence in myself and was insecure about my weight, I let a lot of people bully me. I accepted that fat equals ugly, even though I knew a number of girls I thought were fat and attractive.

"At the place where I worked from the age of nineteen, it soon became common knowledge that I was a virgin after I told a 'friend.' I was also quite odd and shy. I had a crush on one of my friends, and soon it became a running joke, which I was again the butt of. There was a bet: whoever had sex with me would get $2,000. And they kept jokingly increasing the prize pool. I laughed at first and thought it would die, as most bad jokes do. It never did.

"For the next five years, it was ongoing. There were team leaders, managers, and other co-workers all involved in this 'joke.' At the time, if some guy was flirting with me, I'd wonder: Was it for the money or did I look nice that day? It messed with my confidence and my ability to talk to people.

"I had a manager come to me . . . to ask if I wanted to lodge a complaint for bullying. If I had known then what I know now about who was involved and how much it was going to mess me up, I would have done it, because it was sexual harassment and it was bullying, and it never went away."

—*Pandora*

"I was bullied for being ugly for many years, from sixth grade until ninth grade. I had bad skin and wore glasses. I hated myself and what I looked like. I used to wish I could be someone else and wondered what my life would be like if I didn't have bad skin. My mum tried everything to fix my skin."

—*Kristen*

"I got boobs in the fourth grade, so I'm no stranger to these things. Never having had sex in my entire life, I was called a slut."

—Michelle

"Before I lost the weight, I felt invisible, and once I did, I felt that I was constantly scrutinized. Many men I knew acted like I had lost the weight for them and [that] it gave them the right to keep a running commentary on my body."

—Deanna

"Since I developed the body of a woman at an early age, I've had to deal with casual sexual harassment on the streets like any other woman, but nothing out of the ordinary on any of these occasions. Not that sexual harassment on the streets is ordinary and shouldn't be fought against. What I meant is that it's common.

"I've also had to deal with situations in which men and, later, boys of my age tried to kiss me without consent, putting their hands over my body or trying to hold me forcibly. In all of these situations, I felt very uncomfortable and even blamed myself in some. But in the more extreme cases, such as the kisses without consent, I fought and pushed the guy back. But it's awful. Even in the least serious cases, I felt usurped of the right to my own body, violated by such unwanted intimacy."

—Vitoria

"I've been bullied before about my weight. Other kids have made comments about how I'm 'too big' and whatnot. I think I got so tired of being teased about my weight, and that's what started me going down the wrong direction with losing weight."

—Heidi

"Most boys I know think that catcalling is acceptable because they're 'complimenting' girls. But really, it makes them uncomfortable. Girls should learn to stand up to catcallers; they should teach girls that in school if they aren't already taught how by family members.

"Bullying people about their appearance . . . well, I think it's awful, but I have no solution to it, because if you tell an adult, nothing really gets done and the bully just hates you more. I would say stand up to bullies, but it's easier said than done. I know when I was sort of bullied by a couple of girls that I was too scared to do anything, although I wanted to."

—*Alexa*

"It's stupid and pointless, but boys like to tease girls about their image because we don't look like Victoria's Secret models. But we can't even blame them for their thoughts, because that's what they're taught through media, just like girls are taught they have to be . . . models—which is unrealistic."

—*Madeleine*

"I've been bullied since I was six. I've been called names since I can remember: fat, lesbian, weird, stupid, freak, whore, loser, obese, cow. I've got[ten] hit, kicked, had food and water thrown at me, had chemicals and detergents thrown at me and sprayed in my face. People have threatened to kill me after school, people have threatened to set my hair on fire, and I got beaten up twice. Bullies made accusations that I'd stolen knives so I was searched by the police. (And found not guilty!)

"I am a huge advocate for anti-bullying. I've set up a Facebook page that basically helps people talk about their issues and speak their minds."

—*Rebecca*

"I hate how people bully other people. It's disgusting. I am very against bullying."

—Kate

"Bullying is absolutely rampant in our society. Due to my size, I was a victim of it from complete strangers and from members of my family. To stop bullying, I think it is very important to raise children to have so much self-esteem that no one's negative comments can tear them down."

—Jackie

"I used to get bullied a lot, but I realized I was just trying to be someone I'm not. I embarrassed myself a lot because I was trying to be who I thought people wanted me to be. After I started acting like myself, I made friends and the bullying stopped."

—Tanya

Chapter 8
BODY IMAGE AND SELF-ESTEEM

Body image and self-esteem are separate but related concepts. While body image is your mental picture of your body (what you think it looks like and how you feel about it), self-esteem is your judgment about yourself (how much you value and respect yourself). Unfortunately, many of us base our self-esteem solely on our body image. This is a problem. If you feel unhappy with your body, then you are also likely to be unhappy with yourself.

Society places incredible significance on appearance; this is why body image plays such a big factor in the development of high or low self-esteem.

> If your body image starts to become more important than any other aspect of your life, it will interfere with your self-esteem.

Low self-esteem and more serious disorders are caused not only by being unable to achieve body ideals but also by being incredibly invested in appearance.

Here are a couple scenarios.

GIRL A is generally happy with her weight but feels pressure from the media to lose a little. She places great emphasis on academia and profession (education, career); they are more important to her than appearance. Her academic and professional accomplishments contribute more to her self-esteem than her appearance does. Therefore, she is less likely to engage in dieting or disordered eating behaviors.

GIRL B is generally unhappy with her weight due to pressure from the media to be thin. She places great emphasis on appearance above all else. Her appearance contributes more to her self-esteem than anything else. But because the media's body image standards are impossible, she fails to achieve her goal of an ideal body. Therefore, she is more likely to engage in dieting or disordered eating behaviors.

> Many studies have found that by building self-esteem, women can combat the body image ideals they are faced with.

The process of building self-esteem must start with family and other personal relationships (friends, peers, teachers, etc.). The way you're treated by others determines what you learn about your self-worth. This means that if you're treated with respect and love, your self-esteem will be higher and you'll be better equipped to handle the challenges associated with body image. In fact, there is a direct connection between family relationships and the development of eating disorders. If you grow up in a family that makes you feel you don't live up to expectations, then you may be uncertain of your own value and ultimately respond to societal expectations of slimness by developing a disorder. Girls with low self-esteem are more likely to report receiving criticism rather than praise from both parents in comparison to girls with higher self-esteem. In a study on self-esteem commissioned by Dove, 75 percent of girls with low self-esteem reported that when they feel bad about themselves, they engage in negative activities, such as disordered eating, cutting, bullying, smoking, or drinking. In girls with high self-esteem, the number was only 25 percent.

> Self-esteem also has a direct effect on how girls take care of themselves emotionally and physically.

Self-esteem seekers, or those who strive to meet societal expectations, get stuck in the never-ending challenges of reaching for an ideal body image. Girls with low self-esteem feel good about themselves only when they're told that they *are* meeting expectations (for example, when they're told they look skinny or like they've lost weight). This is problematic because validating comments like these could eventually become these girls' only source of positive self-esteem. And if that feeling of increased self-esteem is only temporary, they might start to increasingly use more fat talk or take drastic measures to attain body and beauty ideals.

Self-esteem is a key indicator, or sign, of psychological well-being.

Females with low self-esteem are more likely to be affected by mental health issues, such as depression, anxiety, and eating disorders.

Without positive self-esteem, you might measure your value based only on your appearance and not on the many other great things that make you who you are. If girls could receive more approval from people in their lives and from society, they would develop higher levels of self-esteem and be better equipped against developing mental health issues and eating disorders. In order to develop positive self-esteem, it's crucial to learn to be critical of what you are exposed to in the media and to find positive media sources that encourage a healthy body image.

Getting to Know You

Now it's time to ask yourself some questions and reflect on those answers. Fill in your responses in the provided spaces, or use a personal journal. Be open and honest with yourself. Don't be afraid to explore your thoughts, no matter how delicate or personal they may feel. This is the time for you to recognize your own beauty and learn about yourself.

What type of person do you think others believe you are?

_____

_____

_____

_____

_____

Is your self-esteem mostly based on what other people think of you? How many of those perceived judgments are based on appearance? Explore those perceived qualities that are not based on appearance. These are the abilities that give you the most strength.

_____

_____

_____

_____

_____

_____

"I especially love my stretch marks, I think they are so cool!"

–HAILEY ROBIN MCDOWELL

Chapter at a Glance

- *Body image* is your mental picture of your body.

- *Self-esteem* is how much you value yourself.

- Body image affects self-esteem, so it's crucial to build high self-esteem and a positive body image in order to ward off negative effects of poor body image.

- Self-esteem is affected by personal relationships with family, friends, and others, so it is important that you have a good support system to help you handle social pressures.

- Without healthy self-esteem, a girl may find value from only her appearance.

"I feel like having autism makes me beautiful as I am inspiring other's like myself to do things they wouldn't normally do."

—KELSEY-ROSE
MACDONALD

Average Girls: Thoughts from *Real Girls* on Body Image and Self-Esteem

"Until I find someone who will love me for me, I'm never going to feel beautiful. Our view of our self-worth comes from others, I find."

—*Tanya*

"I just see girls or hear guys talking about their 'hotness' and wonder why I can't have that 'hotness.' I'm insecure, I guess . . ."

—*Alexa*

"I was always told by my dad that I was 'fugly,' or had 'thunder thighs,' or could make things shake when I walked."

—*Karie*

"I learned about my body from my father, and what he told me [was] about what it should be and how it should be prepared for male consumption. I learned to make myself look like what he wanted me to be so that he could consume it. I was a morphing blob of flesh, molding myself into what he found attractive."

—*Leonie*

"I feel rejected by certain men—not so much because I'm not attractive, but because my personality quirks aren't considered attractive to them. This makes me look to my appearance and find fault that I'm not good-looking enough for them to look past appearance at my personality."

—*Kristen*

"I've had people comment on my small breasts since I was about twelve. My parents commented on my small chest growing up, and recently my mother made a bitchy comment that she doesn't know where I got my chest from. I've been bullied about my size and body shape and about being ugly. Growing up, nobody ever told me I was pretty. I was always made to feel ugly and like there was something wrong with me.

"When I turned fourteen and went to a new school, I began to get male attention. This was the first time I ever felt good about myself. I would walk down the street and men of all ages would beep their horns at me. I felt happy and pretty for the first time. Looking back now, as an older person, I know it wasn't good attention. I dressed like your average fourteen-year-old and looked fourteen, but the attention I was getting was mostly from men aged twenty-five to sixty-plus. There are more perverts out there than we'd all care to imagine."

—*Leesha*

"I was always skinny, but I . . . always have been afraid of gaining weight. My mom always used to say, 'Never stop exercising after school, because you'll get fat like me.' She made it seem like it was bad. All my family members were always kind of putting down bigger people by saying they were fat or needed to diet.

"I never acted on my fears because I was small. I just exercised a lot to keep from getting fat, like Mama said. I also think that if the ones I look up to can't love themselves, how can I?"

—*Heather*

"My ex was the only person to actually bully me about being fat, but family members have always compared me to my sisters."

—*Kayla*

"I learned about the female body from my mother."

—Rachel

"I truly believe that society has this idea of what beauty is. It is a size 0 woman that teaches . . . young women that beauty is only skin deep. Sisters, mothers, aunts, etc., need to help and explain to young ladies that the models and stars have money to make themselves perfect; if they didn't look perfect, they wouldn't have a job."

—Wendy

"Young girls need to develop an appreciation for their bodies as forces of action and change before they appreciate those bodies as attractors of male attention. This differentiation starts around age three or four, guided by parents and culture. Sports and physical extracurriculars are a great way to do this early on. After that, a girl has to retrain her own thinking about herself, away from being an object and into being a subject/actor."

—Phoebe

"I suppose my thoughts and ideas about female beauty came from my mom. She's never been smaller than a size 24 that I can remember, and yet she's always exuded self-confidence and landed herself one of the best-looking guys at her high school.

"I think that in the media today, there is a good effort to include 'real' women, but I don't know that it would change a whole lot for today's generation. For those whose moms pressured them to be thin, that's already ingrained in their minds. They are going to end up passing it on to their daughters, whether by their own actions or by their words. I think this subject is something that should be introduced into schools."

—Erin

"I am beautiful and have a strong healthy body. Just because I have a special need doesn't mean I am not confident."

—JESSICA LIEGHFARS-ROTOLO

"I've had people call me fat, even my own flesh-and-blood family, but that didn't seem to affect my thought processes in any way."

—Sahar

"My husband makes me feel beautiful and sexy. He's been with me through thick and thin, pardon the pun."

—Louise

"Knowing that my husband loves my body, regardless of the number on the scale, makes me feel beautiful."

—Morgan

"I was a very thin teen and young woman, 5 foot 9 and weighing 102 to 120 pounds from the ages of sixteen to about thirty-five. I did not become fuller-figured until my late thirties, and now my weight ranges from 185 to 200 pounds. (I'm currently 191 pounds and a size 12/14 US.) I have felt equally beautiful both ways.

"I have been self-assured and had great self-esteem since early childhood, and I thank my mom for this. I have a strong and confident personality. This has carried me far. I don't have the most beautiful face or a perfect body by any means, but I've always been considered very attractive. (I have been a model for over thirty years.) This is due to confidence and a positive sense of self."

—Michelle

"I have a big heart and lots of love for the ones I care most about."

—Jennifer

"My smile draws people in; my personality keeps them around. The eyes are the window to the soul. I have been blessed with so many things that people consider beautiful, but vanity would cancel all that out."

—Rae

"Having babies made me appreciate my body more. I have learned to accept and appreciate my curves. I no longer want to be skinny, but just a healthy version of me."

—Gera

"I learned about female beauty from my mother. She always taught me that you can only love what you were given, because disliking your appearance is a waste of time. I always saw my mother as beautiful, and I still do."

—Jess

"I accept myself and all my weaknesses and strengths as a person. I know that I am who I am because of my family, life experiences, and relationships with people. I like that my body tells me when it needs rest and that, when I pay attention to it, it has the ability to recover on its own. My personality makes people feel that they can trust me. I strive to achieve goals that I have set for myself rather than doing what other people expect of me."

—Sandra

Chapter 9
WHAT TO LOOK FOR
IN THE MEDIA

· ·

"Beauty is not in the face; beauty is a light in the heart."

—*Kahlil Gibran*

The media knows exactly what it's doing when it sends a message to a group of people. We need to pay close attention to *why* certain messages are continually reinforced in the media. Then we can understand *how* the messages relate to our lives. To be able to challenge the media, girls need to practice identifying issues that are present in the media they're exposed to.

In order to help you develop those skills, this and the next chapter contain several questions to help you think and analyze.

As you better recognize what kind of media you allow into your life and how it makes you feel, you will be better able to prepare yourself to fight against those messages and develop a truer sense of who you are—*beautiful* and *real*.

The following are some common ways that different kinds of media perpetuate harmful messages.

Television and Movies

In television shows and movies, female characters are more likely to be attractive and provocatively dressed than male characters. In movies, they more-often appear nude compared to males. Female characters are almost always presented as sexual or sexually appealing; they are often the object of male desire, rather than the subject (the person who is doing something meaningful).

Some examples of shows with this type of female depiction include *The Fast and the Furious* series and *The Bachelor*.

Your turn! List some examples.

_____

_____

_____

_____

_____

_____

How do these depictions make you feel?

_____

_____

_____

_____

_____

_____

Although most female leads still typically possess a thin body type, some examples where women are better depicted as strong and intelligent include *Captain Marvel*, *Noelle*, and *Frozen*. The romantic comedy *Isn't It Romantic* has one of the first plus-size actresses as the lead. As much as these characters are steps in the right direction, it's important to note that all of these leading ladies are white.

What are some examples you can think of? Do you feel that more positive representations allow you to feel better about yourself? What body types would you like to see represented in television and movies?

_____

_____

_____

_____

_____

_____

_____

_____

_____

_____

_____

_____

_____

_____

_____

> "It is important to believe in your dreams."
>
> —KELSEY MOORE

Music Videos

In music videos, female singers and actors are more likely to be physically attractive and provocatively dressed than male musicians or actors. Females are typically portrayed as objects for male-viewing pleasure, and female bodies are positioned in ways that highlight their sexual willingness. The lyrics of many popular songs also sexualize and degrade females.

Examples of music videos that objectify women is Enrique Iglesias's "Move to Miami" or Pitbull's "Don't Stop the Party."

Your turn! List some examples.

_____

_____

_____

_____

_____

_____

_____

_____

_____

Look at the videos you listed. Take special notice if any of the music videos you listed are some of your favorite songs or have particularly catchy tunes. Does the music help you forget what you are viewing?

There aren't many music videos that are body positive, but some do exist. Examples are Lizzo's "My Skin" and Meghan Trainor's "All About That Bass" (even though at some points it could unintentionally come across as putting down women with skinny bodies).

Can you list any music videos that don't sexualize or objectify women?

_____

_____

_____

_____

_____

_____

Was it easy or hard to find these examples in music videos? Do you notice any difference in how these videos make you feel about yourself, as compared to how other videos make you feel?

_____

_____

_____

_____

_____

_____

_____

_____

_____

_____

_____

_____

"I try and find the good in everything that is around me. I've been told that my personality radiates and so does my happiness."

—JENN PELLING

Magazines and Blogs

The messages portrayed in articles and images of magazines and blogs are that being sexually desirable to men is a woman's greatest goal and that an attractive appearance is crucial to sexual, financial, and physical success. Exercise is promoted as a way to improve looks rather than improve health. Advertisements' target is to increase body dissatisfaction in females.

You may read magazine articles that imply these messages with titles along the lines of "How to Get a Supermodel's Butt in Only an Hour" or "The Lazy Girl's Guide to Perfect Abs."

Your turn! List some examples.

_____

_____

_____

_____

_____

_____

_____

_____

_____

_____

_____

_____

Look at your list and think about what how you feel when you see images or articles that fixate on specific ways to achieve society's idea of beauty. Do they motivate you to want to change anything about yourself?

Can you find any articles that make you feel beautiful or empowered by who you already are? List them!

_____

_____

_____

_____

_____

Did you find examples right away, or did you have to search a while to find them? Think about the overall messages in articles and images you searched through—what do you think the goal of the magazines or blogs is with the content they provide to their readers? How does this affect you personally?

_____

_____

_____

_____

_____

_____

_____

_____

_____

"What I like about my body and personality is the extraordinary ability to not only survive trauma, pain, and hardships but also bounce back afterwards."

—FRANKY THOMAS

The Internet

As we discussed earlier, on the internet you can find endless images of thinspiration and fitspiration, as well as pro-ana and pro-mia websites.

A sample thinspiration slogan is "Nothing tastes as good as skinny feels."

Your turn! List some examples.

_____

_____

_____

_____

Something to think about: How often do you find yourself looking to these examples? Do you find them popping up in your feeds without having to search them out? How do they make you feel?

_____

_____

_____

_____

_____

_____

_____

While there are plenty of images on the internet to invoke inadequacy, let's list some examples of celebrities, influencers, images, websites, or groups that inspire girls to love who they are.

_____

_____

_____

_____

_____

_____

A few of my favorites include Instagram influencers like @thebirdspapaya, @own-itbabe, and @bodyposipanda. Hashtags to follow include #normalizenormalbodies and #effyourbeautystandards. A celebrity podcast to listen to would be "Pretty Big Deal" by model Ashley Graham (prettybigdealpodcast.com). And, of course, check out my body-positive blog: www.happydaughter.com.

How do you think you can adjust your internet usage to better surround yourself with positive images?

_____

_____

_____

_____

_____

_____

Cosmetics and Fashion Products

Companies target females to sell them products that will supposedly emphasize their sexuality and make them appear ideally attractive.

Pay close attention to makeup and fashion advertisements and how they make you feel.

In all kinds of advertising, females are more often represented as sexual objects than men; they are frequently placed in submissive positions and clothed for display. Females in ads seem to have power only when they are sexualized in images. Sometimes female bodies even appear dismembered when an image focuses on a body part rather than showing the whole woman. Many of the products promoted in advertisements encourage sexualization or promise to give the customer ideal beauty.

One example of the way women are objectified in this category is the "sexy" Halloween costumes manufactured for teenage girls and women. Companies create sexy versions of normal costumes (sexy devil, sexy nurse, sexy teacher) that are extraordinarily skimpy and, to say the least, unrealistic.

An example of a company that sexualizes women is Victoria's Secret. Their advertisements do not include the many body types that actually purchase their products (though they may publicize that they are including them). Specifically worth mentioning is a campaign they created called "The Perfect Body: Perfect Fit. Perfect Comfort. Perfectly Soft." The statement read like they were body positive, yet all the models in the ad possessed the same skinny waist and big-breasted body type.

Your turn! List some examples.

_____

_____

_____

_____

_____

_____

_____

_____

Have you ever felt the need to prepare or dress yourself in a certain way that made you feel more alluring? Did it give you more confidence? Why do you think that is?

_____

_____

_____

_____

_____

_____

_____

_____

_____

_____

Something to think about: While there are many companies that go overboard in their message that we need their products to feel beautiful, I'm not saying you should never allow yourself to indulge in them. Are there any companies that you support because they are body positive or inclusive of real girls? Some of my favorites include Dove and Aerie, who use a variety of real body types in all of their advertising!

_____

_____

_____

_____

_____

_____

We live in a world that seems to require that we use certain cosmetic or fashion products. How can you indulge in some of these items without allowing them to define your identity? Some examples may include going out in public once a week with little to no makeup on or wearing comfortable clothing styles. (Goodbye, tight jeans. Hello, yoga pants!)

_____

_____

_____

_____

_____

_____

_____

_____

Advertising: The Sum of All Evils

Advertising can be found in all forms of media. Ads appear on the internet and in magazines, on the radio and on television, and even embedded in movies and television shows, where you might barely notice them. As women have begun to take a stand against this type of advertising, some companies (like women's sportswear retailers) have changed their tactics to include women of all shapes and sizes. This is encouraging and should be applauded, but we certainly have a long way to go.

How can you show support to those who show or advertise products for average, real women? How can we teach others to do the same?

_____

_____

_____

_____

_____

_____

_____

_____

_____

> "Real women are fat. And thin. And both, and neither, and otherwise."
>
> —*Hanne Blank*

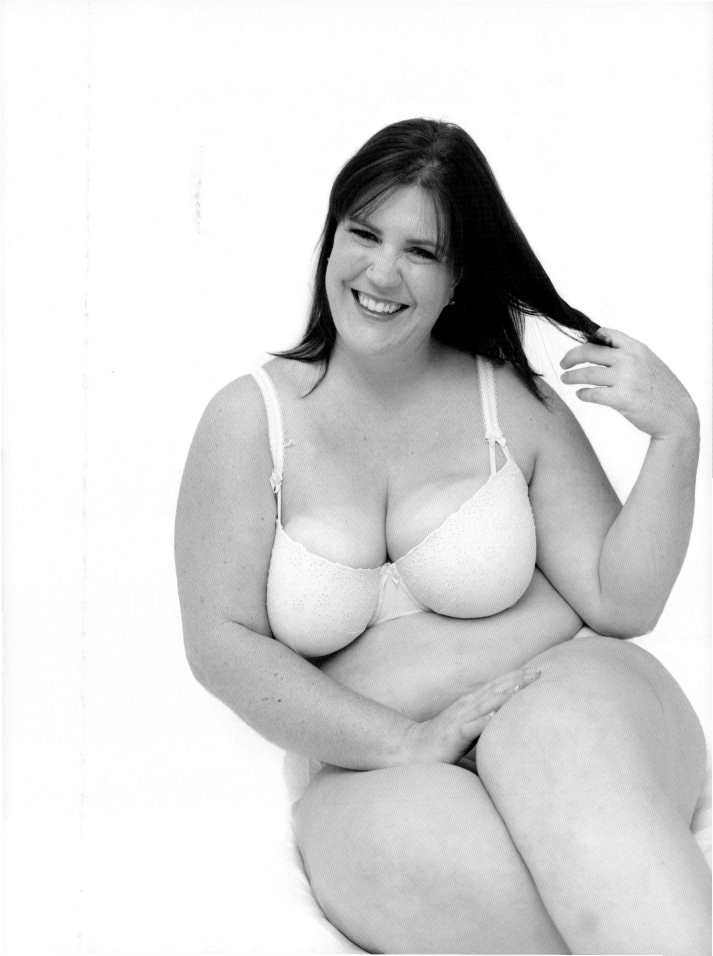

Getting to Know You

Now it's time to ask yourself some questions and reflect on those answers. Fill in your responses in the provided spaces, or use a personal journal. Be open and honest with yourself. Don't be afraid to explore your thoughts, no matter how delicate or personal they may feel. This is the time for you to recognize your own beauty and learn about yourself.

Choose any advertisement featuring a female and answer the following questions about it.

ASK WHAT: What message do you think this advertisement is sending?

_____

_____

_____

_____

ASK WHO: Who is the media targeting? (People of which gender, race, age, background?)

_____

_____

_____

_____

Who is represented in the advertisement?

_____

_____

_____

_____

ASK WHY: Why do you think the media is promoting this message?

_____

_____

_____

_____

_____

ASK HOW: How are females represented in the ad?

_____

_____

_____

_____

_____

How are the females placed and how are they dressed?

_____

_____

_____

_____

_____

If there are any males in the ad, how are they placed and dressed?

_____

_____

_____

_____

_____

How do you feel about this advertisement? Does it make you feel good or bad? Explain.

_____

_____

_____

_____

_____

Imagine you have been chosen to create an advertisement that will feature the *new* and *improved* beauty and body ideal! What message do you want to send in the ad?

_____

_____

_____

_____

_____

Sketch it!

"I like that I am strong, even in my weak moments. I like that I've learned to take care of myself so that I can take care of my family."

—JEN DANCHUK

Chapter at a Glance

- All forms of media can be used to perpetuate negative messages about female bodies.

- Female characters are likely to be attractive and provocatively dressed, as opposed to their male counterparts. (Females are the object; males are the subject.)

- Usually, even when women are represented as powerful and strong, they possess ideal body types.

- Female singers and actors are positioned in ways that highlight their sexual willingness.

- Magazines and blogs showcase articles that fixate on female beauty and present features that promise to correct bodies with certain methods.

- Advertisements exist to create dissatisfaction so that viewers will purchase products that will help them achieve ideal beauty.

- There are positive media examples out there! They can be hard to find, but they're there, and more are greatly needed!

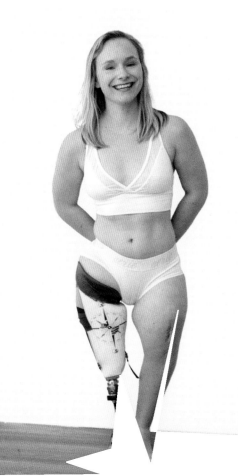

"There are physical scars that show some of those hard times and I wear them as badges of honor that I earned after a hard fight that I won."

—CHRISTINA PICTON

Average Girls: Thoughts from *Real* Girls on What to Look for in the Media

"I challenge media stereotypes by being happy and comfortable in my body. Being a curvy girl, my body isn't deemed as a 'bikini body.' But I have a body and a bikini, so you best believe if media standards tell me I 'shouldn't' wear a bikini, I will anyways. I'll look cute as heck doing it.

"Every time we open social media, we see someone prettier, skinnier, maybe even a better life than us. But that is only just a part of their lives that they choose to share. Why do we spend so much of our free time craving other people's lives? We just need to focus on our own happy. Put that bikini on and be happy."

—*Jess*

"Being a blonde, I . . . have been faced with stereotypes my whole life. The way I deal with it is by staying true to myself and using the negative stereotypes against me to propel myself to challenge it. If blondes are so dumb, how am I graduating from Wilfrid Laurier University with an honors degree in biology and working towards a second degree in nursing?

"As for my personal views on stereotypes portrayed by the media, I make sure to keep an open mind and make my own opinions of people individually based on my experiences. I avoid using molds that have been set out by the media which categorize people based on their race, skin color, hair color, the way they dress, etc."

—*Deanne*

"I challenge media stereotypes by continuing to build my own success. I was a teen mom, got married, and checked all the boxes of what would be a stereotypical success story. The media tells us we need these stereotypical 2.5 kids in suburbia with the trophy wife and the husband who makes good money, but they don't tell you how much of yourself you have to give away to get that dream. I was only 'allowed' to work a little bit, had very little control of my money, was constantly told I needed to lose weight and look more like a 'good wife.' I even got a boob job and worked out insanely so I could fall into that category.

"Eventually I realized the dream I bought into was a lie, and I was in a very toxic place. I left my husband, took my kids, and made sure my business could support us. My life doesn't look like what the media would consider success, but living every day in a way that sets a good example for my children is way more important than what Joe Blow Media thinks of my situation."

—*Beth*

"Challenge people's assumptions and comments. Education is key!"

—*Heather*

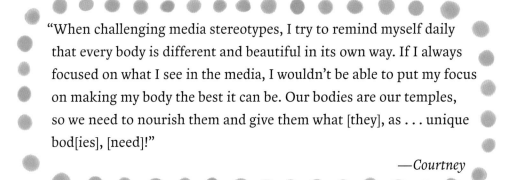

"When challenging media stereotypes, I try to remind myself daily that every body is different and beautiful in its own way. If I always focused on what I see in the media, I wouldn't be able to put my focus on making my body the best it can be. Our bodies are our temples, so we need to nourish them and give them what [they], as . . . unique bod[ies], [need]!"

—*Courtney*

"I challenge media stereotypes by living by my own rules of beauty and owning who I am. The media tells me that I can't be a 'feminine' woman and be smart. Well, I have an undeniable love of the color pink and a university degree with honors that [say] otherwise!

"Women are also expected to be emotional and primarily concerned with relationships—maternal and romantic. Hey, I may cry my eyes out at a cheesy romantic comedy, but that doesn't mean I'm 'weak.' It means I'm a human with the capacity to feel emotion, and that's amazing.

"The media tells women we have to look a certain way in order to be accepted. Once I realized how wrong/unfair/unacceptable/ unobtainable these standards are, I started rebelling against them. Why is it only acceptable that men have hair on their face/legs/ arms/armpits? Women have hair! It's how we're built! Shaving my legs or my armpits is not at the top of my list of priorities. I used to think I had to be hairless in order to be beautiful. Now I'm beautiful regardless of my body hair.

"Also, I don't wear makeup unless I feel like it, but it took a lot of time to work up the courage. After all, it was the media who made me feel like I had to wear makeup in the first place. When I was younger, I 'wouldn't be caught dead' without makeup because I thought that's what women had to do to look pretty. Screw those beauty standards; I'm beautiful with or without makeup.

"Best of all, I don't feel the need to diet to make other people happy. . . . The diet industry would love me to hate my body, but (as it turns out) I don't have to take up less space in the world or shrink myself in order to fill unrealistic standards of beauty. I can love my body and all that it does for me at any size. Ultimately, I challenge media stereotypes by loving myself, regardless of what I look like or who I am."

—*Jessica*

"I think I challenge the constant perfect image in media by remembering that everyone has a story and that a lot of the images we see on social media are fake or Photoshopped. It is important to remember that the so-called perfect women we see in pictures may be very unhappy in real life, so [it is important to remember] not to idolize social images of people we don't 'know.' As long as you are true to yourself and remember that your happiness is all that truly matters."

—*Bronwyn*

"Being a visible minority and a female, I've always felt underrepresented in the media. Recently I've become aware that presence and participation creates possibility! I have used modeling as a way to show photographers that beauty comes in all colors, and to remind myself and others that representation matters."

—*Renee*

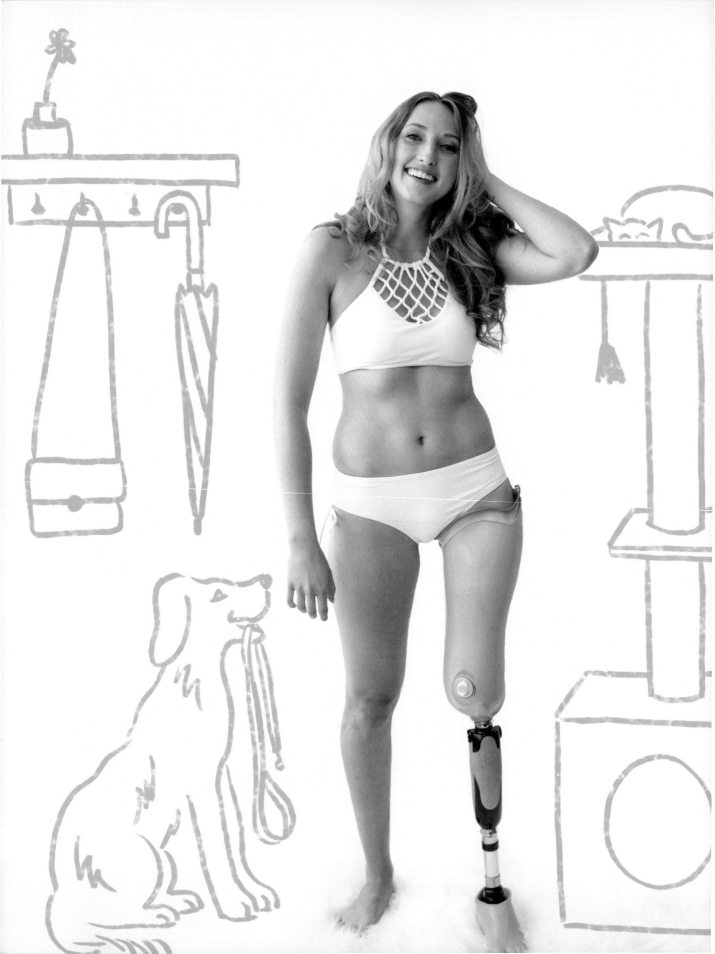

Chapter 10
CHANGING HOW YOU THINK: TEN STEPS TO LOVING YOUR BODY

· ·

1. Forgive yourself.

Once you understand the reasons that you compare and judge yourself and others, remember to forgive yourself for doing so. Because the ideal body image has become so ingrained in our society's way of thinking, we often fail to recognize when we are being hurtful to others and to ourselves. Remember that your negative thoughts were learned from society's ideologies and that you have the power to change this way of thinking—at least in yourself. Do this by taking control of your own thoughts and starting to think about who you really are as a person.

> You are not defined by your size, weight, or looks. *You are defined by the type of person you are and the type of person you want to become.*

Redefine your identity by challenging normal methods of thinking. When you do, you will learn to stop comparing and judging people, and yourself, against societal beauty and body standards.

What can you forgive yourself for?

_____

_____

_____

_____

_____

_____

Who are you right now? Who do you want to be?

_____

_____

_____

_____

_____

_____

_____

2. Think critically.

If you want to redefine your identity, you need to start challenging social norms. A *norm* is a standard of average or proper behavior. As we have discussed, *social norms* are heavily reinforced by mass media. Start challenging the messages that deliberately influence the way we think.

Start asking yourself (and others) questions about *why* the media promotes particular messages. Observe *how* female bodies are represented, and ask yourself *why* they are presented in such a way. *What* is the purpose of particular media messages, and *how* do they make you feel about yourself? *Be aware* of what you are watching, listening to, and reading . . . but remember also to *enjoy* it. If at any point you do not enjoy the media, ask yourself questions about why you are not able to completely enjoy it.

Research the media you are accessing and learn the process of how a media product is created. For example, advertisers selling a line of bathing suits may use Photoshop on the images of their models' bodies. The surface message they want to send is that if you buy their bathing suits, you will look and feel good, but the hidden message is that you need to look a certain way to be considered beautiful by society. On the internet, you will find several articles that show images before and after Photoshop was used to manipulate and change the way the models look.

What would you like to change about the media? What would you like to see from it?

_____

_____

_____

_____

_____

_____

_____

_____

_____

_____

_____

_____

3. Listen.

Listen to what your body is telling you. Our bodies often tell us when we are hungry, tired, or in need of some exercise! *Understanding how you feel in your body is an important part of being physically and mentally healthy.* Remember that everybody is different, so what is good for you may not be the same as what's good for someone else. Do not push yourself to do anything that your body is not comfortable with, and make note of anything that causes you pain or difficulty (physical or emotional) so that you can seek appropriate support, if needed.

What is your body in need of? What is it trying to tell you? What has it been deprived of?

_____

_____

_____

_____

_____

_____

_____

_____

_____

_____

_____

4. Seek support.

It is important to surround yourself with supportive people who will love and care for you, regardless of your appearance. Let go of the people in your life who put you down and make you feel bad about yourself. If the people closest to you are making you feel this way, talk to them about how you feel. Those who truly care about you will work with you on making necessary changes.

Do not hesitate to contact a professional who can provide medical or emotional support for any struggles you are having. There is a professional out there for just about any issue you may have (depression, anxiety, eating disorders, etc.). If you don't know where to start, a local counselor will help point you in the right direction. Counselors are often employed by schools, businesses, and social services. There are lots of ways to connect with them, including through teachers, parents, doctors, and employers.

Who can you talk to about your feelings? Do you currently have any issues that you need specialized help for?

_____

_____

_____

_____

_____

_____

_____

_____

_____

5. Set goals.

It is a great idea to set goals for yourself—as long as they are realistic in terms of what your body can do for you. Remember that attempting to attain an ideal form of beauty or thinness is not a realistic goal; you will only set yourself up for failure.

Realistic physical goals might include eating intuitively (not depriving yourself of the pleasures of food), training for and running a marathon or 5K (at your own pace), and being more active overall (even as little as taking a walk around the mall once a week).

It is important to also set goals that don't relate to the way you look and that do place importance on your mental well-being. Some such realistic goals are reading a great book, taking a social media break, going on a vacation, continuing your education, and challenging yourself to think differently!

What are your short-term and long-term goals?

_____

_____

_____

_____

_____

_____

_____

_____

_____

_____

6. Give thanks.

Our bodies are amazing! It's important to thank them for being so great. Write down all the things your body allows you to do, and consider all that you've accomplished with your body. Some great things your body can do include playing sports, giving hugs, feeling pleasure, enjoying food, laughing, and loving.

Stop fixating on what your body cannot do, and stop thinking about what you cannot change! Remind yourself how amazing you are by writing down your favorite qualities. (Don't focus on just the physical.) Read that list every day to remember that *you are not just your body; your body is the keeper of everything that makes you* you.

List all the things that you love about your body. List all the things that you love about who you are.

_____

_____

_____

_____

_____

_____

_____

_____

_____

_____

7. Treat yourself.

Every once in a while, remember to treat yourself to an activity that you enjoy. The more you remember to reward yourself for being you, the happier you will be!

One of the best times to treat yourself is when you're feeling sad. Think about what makes you happy. Treat activities might include getting a haircut, going out for dinner, making a trip to the mall, having a night out with your friends and family, or taking a bubble bath. When you take care of yourself and indulge a little, you *send yourself the message that you and your body are worthy.*

What is your favorite treat? What do you enjoy doing? How can you incorporate these activities more into your life on a regular basis?

_____

_____

_____

_____

_____

_____

_____

_____

_____

_____

_____

_____

8. Dress for comfort.

Nothing makes me feel more comfortable in my own skin than wearing something that feels good on my body! If you wear clothing that you feel physically comfortable in, you will start to feel comfortable in your body. Remember to purchase clothes that fit the body you have, that look good to you, and that feel good! Clothing is a great way to express how you feel, so remember, *size is only a number, and comfort creates confidence (in mind and body).*

What is your favorite outfit? Describe what it looks like and how it makes you feel.

_____

_____

_____

_____

_____

_____

_____

_____

_____

_____

_____

_____

9. Encourage yourself and others.

Instead of discouraging yourself with thoughts about how you're unable to attain ideal beauty standards, *encourage yourself with positive thinking*. Remind yourself that *you are not defined by the way you look*. A great way to feel positive about yourself is to help others feel positive about themselves! Tell your loved ones why you think they're amazing. You will start to feel that you're amazing too.

List the people who care about you and support you. What makes them so special? Don't forget to tell them how you feel!

_____

_____

_____

_____

_____

_____

_____

_____

_____

_____

_____

_____

10. When in doubt, read this book.

I hope that when girls are feeling down, they can pick up this book, look at images that make them feel good, and read information that will help them challenge the images in the media that promote body dissatisfaction.

Stop using fat talk, and replace your body hatred with words of *encouragement* and *support*. Next time you feel the urge to say something like "I feel fat," instead say, "I feel average." Fat is not the problem; society's idea that it is is the problem. Remember that fat is not a feeling! Get to the bottom of why you "feel fat" by asking yourself what is actually affecting your mood and what you can do about it. The answer might be something like "I feel down because I just read a magazine and my body type is not represented in it. I feel like I don't fit into the standards of the magazine I'm reading. This makes me feel bad about my body. I have a right to feel upset that my body is not represented. I'm going to do something to make myself feel good. I'm going to stop reading this magazine."

Seek out forms of positive media and surround yourself with resources that challenge body ideals. Some positive media on the internet can be found by searching for "before and after Photoshop," "anti-thinspo," or "positive body image" articles and images. You can never have enough positive body image resources, so be encouraged to seek them out, or create your own! Just remember to *read, watch, and listen to things that make you feel good about yourself*.

How do you feel after reading this book? Any future plans?

_____

_____

_____

_____

"It's not what you say out of your mouth that determines your life, it's what you whisper to yourself that has the most power."
—*Robert T. Kiyosaki*

"I feel beautiful when I'm surrounded with people I love and when I do things that I love."

—ANGEL LACANILAO

Average Girls: Thoughts from *Real Girls* on Loving Your Body

"I feel beautiful when I am comfortable in what I'm wearing and I'm spending time outside. Sunshine and fresh air make me happy—and when I'm happy, I feel beautiful."

—*Kimberly*

"What makes me happy is a new hairstyle or a smile from a friend. I love my smile."

—*Gisel*

"Beautiful women are women who are beautiful on the inside. They help others and are always kind, even if their appearance isn't always great. I make myself beautiful when I help out others who need help. Who cares what you look like on the outside?"

—*Heaven*

"What makes me feel beautiful is when I am doing something I truly love, like art, theater, or music. I feel beautiful when I think about all the things I can do in life—and none of it comes from what I look like. I love my legs because they can take me places! They let me move around and dance and travel, and do all the things that I love.

"One thing I love about my personality is that I don't like to judge other people. It's weird, because I'm constantly judging myself, but I absolutely will not judge other people. I think everyone is beautiful and perfect the way they are. They don't have to lose weight or look a certain way to be amazing and beautiful."

—*Heidi*

"Beauty is someone's ability to make you feel happy or good about yourself. A beautiful person radiates self-respect and self-love. Sometimes putting makeup on and doing my hair make me feel more beautiful. Sometimes being around people who love me for who I am makes me feel beautiful."

—*Claira*

"I feel beautiful when I'm walking naked around my apartment. I feel beautiful during sex. I feel beautiful when I get dressed up just for myself. I love my breasts, my skin, my dimples, my eyes, and my smile. My personality? I'm a total introvert, so I love that people have to know me and get close to me to appreciate me. I like that I'm friendly and kind."

—*Jessica*

"I feel beautiful when my hair is all done, my makeup is done nicely, I have a cute outfit on, and I know people are going to like it. I think I have nice eyes—even though they're just brown, I find them pretty. I also like how I can take a joke and make jokes."

—*Madeleine*

"I feel beautiful if I have done something nice. I also feel beautiful when I've done something new with my appearance or have a new outfit that I enjoy. I like that I have also been physically strong. I prefer my body when I am at a healthy weight . . . and have muscle tone. I like my sense of humor, my work ethic (I am driven and highly motivated), my charisma, and I think I am intelligent."

—*Nicole*

"A beautiful woman is very kind, selfless, and would do anything to help somebody."

—*Rebecca*

"I learned about female beauty after battling for years with my eating disorder. I unfortunately let societal standards and others' opinions define my beauty and self-worth. I struggle in trying *not* to strive for that 'ideal' standard of society. I think a beautiful woman is confident in herself. She is typically outgoing, has a solid sense of herself and her values, and is not defined by societal standards, nor does she look to others to measure her self-worth."

—*Nicole*

"A beautiful woman has a true smile—one that makes her eyes look sparkly."

—*Hailey*

"How can we define beauty? Every woman is beautiful. It's what's on the inside that matters. I love that I'm happy with my body. I'm not skinny. I am healthy. If I want to eat a whole pizza, I will. I'm a very honest and caring person."

—*Lauren*

I really believe that beauty shines through on a woman's face. What makes me feel beautiful [are] simple things. A compliment from a stranger. A pretty dress I really like. My little girl telling me she thinks I'm pretty. Or my ability to look in the mirror and point out the things I like."

—*Jackie*

"Every single woman
has value and deserves
to feel that they belong
and have worth."

—LARISSA LEONARD

"A beautiful woman is confident. She knows who she is, what she wants, what her value is, and what she deserves—or at least she's committed to figuring it out. She's not ashamed of her body, not caring how it looks, and she's in charge of it. Whether she uses her body image to attract attention or just for her own pleasure doesn't matter; it is her choice. She's an agent in her own body image and definition of beauty. A beautiful woman is beautiful for who she is, for her values and beliefs—for being a woman."

—*Vitoria*

"The most beautiful women in my life are a little unique: curvy, confident, creative, a bit on the wild side. Probably reminiscent of my mum."

—*Louise*

"I feel beautiful when I look in the mirror and concentrate on the aspects of my face that I love, rather than my flaws. To me, a beautiful woman is confident in her body and her mind. She doesn't flaunt, but she's not afraid to show off her sexy side."

—*Emily*

"When someone notices me without makeup on, I like the thought of being loved for me. I like that I'm not too skinny anymore. I like my legs. I like that I laugh a lot, and that I stand up for myself and others when I need to."

—*Dalton*

"I make myself beautiful by being me."

—*Nigela*

"To me, a beautiful woman has a chubby body, a round face, and fat arms and legs. I learned about female beauty from television, magazines, and books when I was growing up, and because I lived in a family of fat women. I found that the women I saw in the media were different from the women in my life. I still think some celeb[rity] women have lovely smiles and look beautiful, but when I think of a beautiful woman, I picture someone like Kirsten Vangsness, who (to me) is the epitome of beautiful.

"How do I make myself beautiful? I don't. I have just come to accept myself. I think at best, I am pretty. The only time I have ever felt beautiful was one night when I was walking down a hotel hallway, coming back from dinner with my boyfriend. I was in jeans and a T-shirt, nothing fancy. But at that moment, I felt like the most beautiful woman in the world.

"What makes me feel beautiful? Putting on a nice piece of clothing, styling my hair a bit differently. Maybe putting on some eyeliner for a change. To have my boyfriend hold my hand as we walk down the street and see his smile as he looks at me like I am the only person in the world."

—*Pandora*

"To me, beauty isn't a way I make myself look. It's a feeling."

—*Erin*

"A beautiful woman is confident, smiles most of the time, stands up tall, embraces her natural beauty, genuinely cares for others, and has something she's passionate about. I learned about female beauty by becoming a high school senior photographer. The more I met young women who were coming to me to feel beautiful, the more I defined what female beauty means to me."

—*Kimberly*

"I learned that the characteristics of a beautiful woman are those that come from within: genuineness, truthfulness, honesty, kindness, and appreciation."

—*Sherry*

"Beautiful woman have poise and confidence. All women are beautiful just for being themselves and having flaws. I've learned about female beauty by communicating with others. I've never really met an ugly girl."

—*Pearl*

"A beautiful woman is radiant in her own skin, powerful, and compassionate to herself and others."

—*Phoebe*

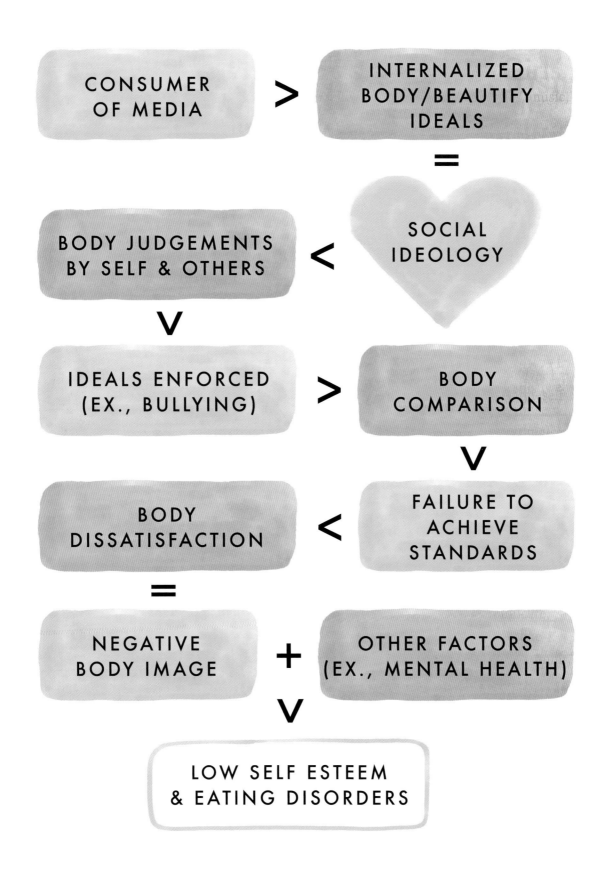

A FINAL NOTE
FROM THE AUTHOR

· ·

This project would not have been complete without getting in front of the camera myself. It has been so long in the making that I've updated my image for the book four times. Ultimately, I've decided to include all of the images taken because I want to highlight that our bodies are constantly changing. In one of the images, I'm four months postpartum; in another, I am four months pregnant; and in the others, I am just happy in the always-changing body that allowed me the privilege of having two children.

We need to be proud of what our bodies can do and how they adapt to our changing lives. Whether our bodies change because of illness, amputation, surgery, pregnancy, or just routine aging, our bodies always adapt. What we need to do now is adapt our minds. We need to embrace our "flaws" and strive for balance and enjoyment in all of our lives.

I want to thank all the amazing women who participated in the making of this book.

Without all of you, this project would not have been possible. Your stories and dedication to changing the minds of today and tomorrow are just what our society needs to improve body confidence.

There are far too many issues that coincide with idealizing the female body. Let's start believing that *every body is beautiful* and recognize that we are more similar than we think. Focus on what you can achieve and what your body can do, and the possibilities will be endless.

This is for you (insert your name here!) . . . as well as Adrienne Ressler, Alanna, Alexa, Alli, Alyssa, Amanda, Ana, Angel, Anna, Arielle, Ashton, Beth Marchant, Beverlyn, Brandie, Briana, Brittany, Bronwyn, Caitlynn, Candice, Casey, Cass, Cassie-lynn, Catherine Chen, Chantel, Chelsea, Cheyenne, Chrissy, Christina, Christine, Claira, Claire, Connie, Courtney, Cupcake, Dalton, Danielle, Deanna, Deanne, Deziree,

DramaWay, Emily, Emmy, Erika, Erika, Erin, Francie, Genni, Gera, Gisel, Gloria, Hailey, Hanan, Hanna, Heather, Heather Hogendoorn, Heaven, Heidi, Jackie, Jade, Jelynne, Jenn, Jenni, Jennifer, Jessica, Jessica Camboia, Jessica Ross, Jodi, Karie, Kat, Kate, Kathleen, Kay, Kayla, Kayleigh, Kelly, Kelsey, Kimberly, Kirsten Haglund, Kitty, Kristen, Krystal, Larissa, Latoya, Laura, Lauren, Laurie Duersch, Leesha, Leigh-Anne, Leonie, Leonie, Leslie, Lily, Lina, Lizz, Lorna, Louise, Lucy, Lyndsay, Lynn, Mackenzie, Madeleine, Madison, Mandy, Megan, Melanie, Melissa, Michelle, Mikayla, Monica, Morgan, Moriah, Nadia, Natacha, Nicole, Nigela, Pandora, Pearl, Phoebe, Rachel, Rae, Rebecca, Renee, Sahar, Sam, Samantha, Sandra, Sara, Sarah, Sarana, Sasha, Shar, Sherry, Sierra, Sonya, Sophie, Stella, Stephanie, Sugandh, Sunny, Tamara, Tammy, Tanya, Tina, Tymika, Valerie, Vitoria, Wendy, and anyone who chose to remain anonymous.

xo, Emily Lauren Dick

GLOSSARY

· ·

ANOREXIA ATHLETICA: an eating disorder in which one compulsively exercises to feel in control.

ANOREXIA NERVOSA: an eating disorder in which one has an intense fear of becoming fat or gaining weight, even when they are underweight, accompanied by extreme measures of weight loss.

ATYPICAL ANOREXIA: an eating disorder that fits the criteria for anorexia except that weight remains in acceptable ranges, though the body may be in a state of malnourishment.

AVERAGE: ordinary, mediocre, common, normal, or (sometimes) inferior.

AVERAGE GIRL: a normal girl who feels common or mediocre and who struggles with not being considered ideal by society. An Average Girl represents all girls who feel their bodies don't fit into society's standards but are, nonetheless, unique.

BINGE EATING DISORDER: an eating disorder in which one eats large amounts of food in a short period of time while feeling that they can't stop eating.

BODY DISSATISFACTION: being unhappy with one's body and appearance.

BODY DYSMORPHIC DISORDER: a disorder in which one has irrational concerns about a part of their body.

BODY IMAGE: a person's idea of how others see their body.

BODY POSITIVE: the idea that all bodies are are good bodies. All bodies are worthy of love and respect, and all bodies are beautiful.

BODY POSITIVITY: Body Positivity promotes no body shaming of any kind. The Body Positivity Movement stemmed from the Fat Acceptance Movement, which developed in response to fat-shaming culture and the discrimination of people based on their weight and size.

BODY NEUTRAL: knowing that your body does not define your worth, without the pressure of loving the way your body looks. An in-between place for appreciating your body and knowing that your value has nothing to do with your appearance.

BULIMIA NERVOSA: an eating disorder in which one has episodes of binge eating (eating larger amounts than most people would eat) and then purging (ridding the body of the food to avoid gaining weight).

BULLYING: the act of frightening, threatening, or hurting another person physically or mentally.

DEPRESSION: a mood disorder characterized by extreme sadness, among other symptoms.

DIET: a special regimen of eating and drinking sparingly to reduce one's weight.

DIET (the true meaning): what one eats and drinks daily.

EATING DISORDER: a mental illness characterized by serious disturbances in eating behaviors.

FAT TALK: negative statements about one's body made in everyday conversation. Fat talk reinforces thin ideals.

FITSPIRATION (OR FITSPO): images with text used as inspiration to stay thin or become thin by way of fitness and exercise.

HETEROSEXUAL: a person sexually attracted to people of the opposite sex.

IDEAL: a standard of perfection or excellence.

IDEOLOGY: a set or system of ideas and ideals held by a group.

INTERNALIZE: to incorporate the values, ideas, attitudes, and behaviors of a dominant group into one's identity.

JUDGMENT: an opinion or conclusion about someone or something.

MEDIA: means of communication that reach many people (television, movies, music, magazines, the internet, etc.).

MENTAL DISORDER (OR MENTAL ILLNESS): a condition in which normal psychological functions are impaired by disorganized emotions and thoughts.

ORTHOREXIA: an informal diagnosis for disordered eating in which sufferers are obsessive about eating healthy, which can lead to nutritional deficiencies and illness.

PHOTOSHOP: computer software that allows one to digitally alter a photographic image.

PRO-ANA: the promotion of behaviors related to anorexia nervosa.

PRO-MIA: the promotion of behaviors related to bulimia nervosa.

SELF-COMPARISON: to examine any differences or similarities between oneself and others.

SELF-CRITICISM: evaluating oneself for faults and weaknesses.

SELF-ESTEEM: the amount of self-respect and satisfaction one has for oneself.

SEXUAL ASSAULT: unwanted sexual activity done by one person to another.

SEXUAL HARASSMENT: uninvited and unwanted verbal or physical behavior of a sexual nature.

SOCIAL MEDIA: websites and online communities people use to communicate, network, and share information, ideas, personal messages, and other content (like videos). Some examples are Facebook, Instagram, Pinterest, Snapchat, TikTok, Tumblr, and Twitter.

SUICIDE: taking one's own life voluntarily and intentionally.

THINSPIRATION (OR THINSPO): images with text used as inspiration to become thin.

NOTES

....

Introduction

Marilyn Monroe, quoted in Jean M. Grow and Joyce M. Wolburg, "Selling Truth: How Nike's Advertising to Women Claimed a Contested Reality," *Advertising & Society Review* 7, no. 2 (2006), doi:10.1353/asr.2006.0025. The quote was used in 1991 as part of a Nike ad campaign run by Nike's chief copywriter at the time, Janet Champ. A copy of the ad can be found at the provided source.

Chapter 1: Body Image and Learning the Way

Canadian Population Health Initiative, *Women's Health Surveillance Report: A Multi-dimensional Look at the Health of Canadian Women* (Ottawa: Canadian Institute for Health Information, 2003), https://secure.cihi.ca/free_products/CPHI_WomensHealth_e.pdf.

"Our Research," Dove, accessed April 23, 2020, https://www.dove.com/us/en/stories/about-dove/our-research.html. Findings were pulled from a study by Dove called "The Real Truth about Beauty: Revisited."

Mia Foley Sypeck, James J. Gray, and Anthony H. Ahrens, "No Longer Just a Pretty Face: Fashion Magazines' Depictions of Ideal Female Beauty from 1959 to 1999," *International Journal of Eating Disorders* 36, no. 3 (2004): 342–47.

Hayley K. Dohnt and Marika Tiggemann, "Body Image Concerns in Young Girls: The Role of Peers and Media Prior to Adolescence," *Journal of Youth and Adolescence* 35, no. 2 (February 2006): 135–45.

Blye Frank, as quoted in "Fact Sheet: Moving Girls into Confidence," Canadian Women's Foundation, updated October 2013, https://www.canadianwomen.org/sites/canadianwomen.org/files/FactSheet-Girls-ACTIVE.pdf. See also https://canadianwomen.org/the-facts/barriers-for-girls/ for additional information and statistics on challenges girls face.

Helga Dittmar, Emma Halliwell, and Suzanne Ive, "Does Barbie Make Girls Want to Be Thin? The Effect of Experimental Exposure to Images of Dolls on the Body Image of 5- to 8-Year-Old Girls," *Developmental Psychology* 42, no. 2 (2006): 283–92.

Kevin I. Norton, Timothy S. Olds, Scott Olive, and Stephen Dank, "Ken and Barbie at Life Size," *Sex Roles* 34, no. 3–4 (February 1996): 290.

Margo Maine, *Body Wars: Making Peace with Women's Bodies* (Carlsbad, CA: Gürze Books, 2000), 210. BMI was calculated by the author.

"If Barbie Were Real," infographic, "Dying to Be Barbie: Eating Disorders in Pursuit of the Impossible," Rehabs.com, accessed April 30, 2020, https://www.rehabs.com/explore/dying-to-be-barbie/.

Maine, *Body Wars*, 210.

"If Barbie Were Real."

"Beauty and Body Image in the Media," Media Awareness Network, 2008, www.media-awareness.ca/english/issues/stereotyping/women_and_girls/women_beauty.cfm, as cited in "Beauty and Body Image in the Media," Battered Women's Support Services, June 13, 2011, https://www.bwss.org/beauty-and-body-image-in-the-media/.

"Beauty and Body Image in the Media."

American Psychological Association, Task Force on the Sexualization of Girls, *Report of the APA Task Force on the Sexualization of Girls* (Washington, DC: American Psychological Association, 2007), 13, http://www.apa.org/pi/women/programs/girls/report-full.pdf.

American Psychological Association, *Report of the APA Task Force*, 13–14.

Carolyn Gorman, "Maternal Transmission of Body Image in School-Aged Children," *Undergraduate Review* 3 (2007): 15–19.

Chapter 2: The Media

American Psychological Association, Task Force on the Sexualization of Girls, *Report of the APA Task Force on the Sexualization of Girls* (Washington, DC: American Psychological Association, 2007), 41, http://www.apa.org/pi/women/programs/girls/report-full.pdf.

Jean Kilbourne, in Sut Jhally, dir., *Killing Us Softly 3: Advertising's Image of Women* (Northampton, MA: Media Education Foundation, 1999), DVD.

Naomi Wolf, *The Beauty Myth: How Images of Beauty Are Used Against Women* (William Morrow, 1991; New York: HarperCollins, 2002), 187. Citation refers to the HarperCollins edition.

Wolf, *The Beauty Myth*, 184.

Dawn H. Currie, *Girl Talk: Adolescent Magazines and Their Readers* (Toronto: University of Toronto Press, 1999).

"Body Image—Girls," MediaSmarts, accessed May 4, 2020, https://mediasmarts.ca/body-image/body-image-girls.

Jung-Hwan Kim and Sharron J. Lennon, "Mass Media and Self-Esteem, Body Image, and Eating Disorder Tendencies," *Clothing and Textiles Research Journal* 25, no. 1 (2007): 3–23.

"Women in the Media: Give the Stereotypes a Makeover," Dove, November 1, 2016, https://www.dove.com/us/en/dove-self-esteem-project/help-for-parents/media-and-celebrities/women-in-the-media.html. Findings were pulled from a study called "Body Image: An Introduction to Advertising and Body Image."

Chapter 3: Self-Improvement

"Girls' Attitudes Survey," Girlguiding, 2016, https://www.girlguiding.org.uk/globalassets/docs-and-resources/research-and-campaigns/girls-attitudes-survey-2016.pdf. All of Girlguiding's girls' attitude surveys can be found at https://www.girlguiding.org.uk/girls-making-change/girls-attitudes-survey/.

"Body Image: Introduction," MediaSmarts, accessed April 23, 2020, https://mediasmarts .ca/body-image/body-image-introduction.

Daniel Clay, Vivian L. Vignoles, and Helga Dittmar, "Body Image and Self-Esteem among Adolescent Girls: Testing the Influence of Sociocultural Factors," *Journal of Research on Adolescence* 15, no. 4 (November 2005): 473.

American Psychological Association, Task Force on the Sexualization of Girls, *Report of the APA Task Force on the Sexualization of Girls* (Washington, DC: American Psychological Association, 2007), 4, http://www.apa.org/pi/women/programs/ girls/report-full.pdf.

Victoria Rideout and Michael B. Robb, *The Common Sense Census: Media Use By Tweens and Teens* (San Francisco: Common Sense Media, 2019), 5, http://www.common-sensemedia.org/sites/default/files/uploads/research/2019-census-8-to-18-ke y-findings-updated.pdf.

American Psychological Association, *Report of the APA Task Force*, 3.

Jean Kilbourne, in Sut Jhally, dir., *Killing Us Softly 4: Advertising's Image of Women* (Northampton, MA: Media Education Foundation, 2010), DVD.

Nancy Etcoff, *Survival of the Prettiest: The Science of Beauty* (New York: Anchor Books, 2000), 68–69.

Michael F. Jacobson and Laurie Ann Mazur, *Marketing Madness: A Survival Guide for a Consumer Society* (Boulder, CO: Westview Press, 1995), 75.

Eating Disorder Foundation, cited by Kelsey Miller, "Study: Most Girls Start Dieting by Age 8," Refinery29, January 26, 2015, https://www.refinery29.com/en-us/2015/01/81288/ children-dieting-body-image.

Silvia Knobloch-Westerwick and Josselyn Crane, "A Losing Battle: Effects of Prolonged Exposure to Thin-Ideal Images on Dieting and Body Satisfaction," *Communication Research* 39, no. 1 (2012): 79–102.

Francine Grodstein, Rachel Levine, Lisa Troy, Terri Spencer, Graham A. Colditz, and Meir J. Stampfer, "Three-Year Follow-Up of Participants in a Commercial Weight Loss Program: Can You Keep It Off?", *Archives of Internal Medicine* 156, no. 12 (1996): 1302.

Knobloch-Westerwick and Crane, "A Losing Battle."

Lynn Carol Miller and Cathryn Leigh Cox, "For Appearances' Sake: Public Self-Consciousness and Makeup Use," *Personality and Social Psychology Bulletin* 8, no. 4 (December 1982): 748–51.

Adrienne Ressler, telephone interview with the author, March 2013.

Chapter 4: Self-Comparison and Fat Talk

Marika Tiggemann, "Media Exposure, Body Dissatisfaction and Disordered Eating: Television and Magazines Are Not the Same!", *European Eating Disorders Review* 11, no. 5 (March 2003): 418–30.

Iyanla Vanzant, *Forgiveness: 21 Days to Forgive Everyone for Everything* (Carlsbad, CA: Smiley Books, 2013), 214.

Mimi Nichter, *Fat Talk: What Girls and Their Parents Say about Dieting* (Cambridge, MA: Harvard University Press, 2001).

Adrienne Ressler, "Perspectives on Body Image," *Perspectives* (2015): 13–15, https://renfrewcenter.com/sites/default/files/PERSPECTIVES.pdf.

Marika Tiggemann and Amy Slater, "Thin Ideals in Music Television: A Source of Social Comparison and Body Dissatisfaction," *International Journal of Eating Disorders* 35, no. 1 (January 2004): 48–58.

Lynda G. Boothroyd, Martin J. Tovée, and Thomas V. Pollet, "Visual Diet versus Associative Learning as Mechanisms of Change in Body Size Preferences," *PLOS One* 7, no. 11 (November 2012): e48691.

Chapter 5: Thinspiration

Victoria Stonebridge, "Thinspiration: New Media's Influence on Girls with Eating Disorders" (master's thesis, Rowan University, 2011), https://rdw.rowan.edu/etd/29/.

Stonebridge, "Thinspiration."

Thintillyoubreak, "nothing but skinny please," Tumblr, September 3, 2016, https://thintillyoubreak.tumblr.com/post/140746689819/i-hate-this-to-eat-is-to-die-and-to-starve-is-to.

Laci Green, in lacigreen, "Fat Shame" (video description), YouTube, May 17, 2012, https://www.youtube.com/watch?v=8XhTA4xOxCc.

Victoria Gigante, "The Secret & Silent Killer behind Thinspiration," Psych Central, updated July 8, 2018, https://psychcentral.com/blog/the-secret-silent-killer-behind-thinspiration.

Adrienne Ressler, telephone interview with the author, March 2013.

Ressler, telephone interview.

Stonebridge, "Thinspiration."

Chapter 6: Mental Health

Mood Disorders Society of Canada, "Symptoms of Depression," Depression Hurts, accessed April 20, 2020, http://www.depressionhurts.ca/en/about/symptoms.aspx.

"Causes of Depression," WebMD, accessed April 20, 2020, https://www.webmd.com/depression/guide/causes-depression#1.

Girls Action Foundation, *Girls in Canada Today: National Opinion Poll and Report on the Status of Girls* (Montréal: Girls Action Foundation, 2011), 2, https://www.yumpu.com/en/document/read/22821299/read-the-full-report-girls-in-canada-today-girls-action-foundation. See also "Special Considerations for the Girl Child," Canadian Bar Association, www.cba.org/Publications-Resources/Practice-Tools/Child-Rights-Toolkit/theChild/Girl-Child#fn8.

Sabrina R. Hamilton, "The Relationship between Perceived Body Image and Depression: How College Women See Themselves May Affect Depression," *Student Journal of Psychological Science* 1, no. 1 (2008): 13–20.

Girls Action Foundation, *Girls in Canada Today*, 9.

Girls Action Foundation, *Girls in Canada Today*, #. [Page number?]

Hamilton, "The Relationship between Perceived Body Image and Depression," 13; and Maurizio Pompili, Paolo Girardi, Giulia Tatarelli, Amedeo Ruberto, and Roberto Tatarelli, "Suicide and Attempted Suicide in Eating Disorders, Obesity and Weight-Image Concern," *Eating Behaviors* 7, no. 4 (November 2006): 384–94.

Hamilton, "The Relationship between Perceived Body Image and Depression," 15.

P. F. Sullivan, "Mortality in Anorexia Nervosa," *American Journal of Psychiatry* 152, no. 7 (July 1995): 1073–74. See also "Eating Disorder Statistics," ANAD, accessed May 1, 2020, https://anad.org/education-and-awareness/about-eating-disorders/eating-disorders-statistics.

"Busting the Myths about Eating Disorders," National Eating Disorders Association, February 22, 2018, https://www.nationaleatingdisorders.org/busting-myths-about-eating-disorders.

"Understanding Anorexia—The Basics," WebMD, accessed April 20, 2020, https://www.webmd.com/mental-health/eating-disorders/anorexia-nervosa/understanding-anorexia-basics; and "Bulimia Nervosa," WebMD, accessed April 20, 2020, https://www.webmd.com/mental-health/eating-disorders/bulimia-nervosa/mental-health-bulimia-nervosa#1.

Suzanne F. Abraham, "Dieting, Body Weight, Body Image and Self-Esteem in Young Women: Doctors' Dilemmas," *Medical Journal of Australia* 178, no. 12 (June 2003): 607.

Kelly L. Klump, Cynthia M. Bulik, Walter H. Kaye, Janet Treasure, and Edward Tyson, "Academy for Eating Disorders Position Paper: Eating Disorders Are Serious Mental Illnesses," *International Journal of Eating Disorders* 42, no. 2 (2009): 100.

Jane Morris and Sara Twaddle, "Anorexia Nervosa," *BMJ* (2007), https://doi.org/10.1136/bmj.39171.616840.BE.

"General Information," National Eating Disorder Information Centre, accessed April 20, 2020, https://nedic.ca/general-information/.

Anita Jansen, Tom Smeets, Carolien Martijn, and Chantal Nederkoorn, "I See What You See: The Lack of a Self-Serving Body-Image Bias in Eating Disorders," *British Journal of Clinical Psychology* 45 (2006): 134.

Adrienne Ressler, telephone interview with the author, March 2013.

"Women and Anxiety," Anxiety and Depression Association of America (ADAA), accessed April 30, 2020, https://adaa.org/find-help-for/women/anxiety.

C. M. Bulik, P. F. Sullivan, J. I. Fear, P. R. Joyce, "Eating Disorders and Antecedent Anxiety Disorders: A Controlled Study," *Acta Psychiatrica Scandinavica* 96 (November 1997): 101–07.

Abraham, "Dieting, Body Weight, Body Image and Self-Esteem in Young Women," #. [Page number?]

"Eating Disorders, Body Image and Self-Esteem," HealthQuest, Morneau Shepell fgi, 2005, 9, http://www.shepellfgi.com/EN-CA/Employees%20and%20Families/Wellness%20Articles/Healthy%20Living/pdf/eating_disorders_ws.pdf.

American Psychiatric Association, *Diagnostic and Statistical Manual of Mental Disorders, 5th ed. (DSM-5)* (Arlington, VA: American Psychiatric Association, 2013), 307.59 (f50.8).

"Eating Disorders, Body Image and Self-Esteem."

Abraham, "Dieting, Body Weight, Body Image and Self-Esteem in Young Women," #. [Page number?]

"Medical Issues from Anorexia, Bulimia and Other Eating Disorders," Bulimia.com, updated June 11, 2018, http://www.bulimia.com/topics/medical-issues.

"Body Dysmorphic Disorder," WebMD, accessed April 20, 2020, https://www.webmd.com/mental-health/mental-health-body-dysmorphic-disorder#1.

"Body Dysmorphic Disorder."

"Binge Eating Disorder," National Eating Disorder Information Centre, accessed April 20, 2020, https://nedic.ca/eating-disorders-treatment/binge-eating-disorder/.

"Informal Definitions," "Types of Eating Disorders," National Eating Disorder Information Centre, accessed April 20, 2020, https://nedic.ca/eating-disorders-treatment/.

Stephanie Thorton, "Supporting Individuals with Orthorexia Nervosa," *British Journal of School Nursing* 13, no. 6 (2018): 302–04.

Megan Jones and Tess Brown, "Why Early Intervention for Eating Disorders Is Essential," National Eating Disorders Association, accessed April 30, 2020, https://www.nationaleatingdisorders.org/blog/why-early-intervention-eating-disorders-essential.

"Eating Disorders Facts and Statistics," Body Image Therapy Center, accessed April 20, 2020, http://www.thebodyimagecenter.com/education-awareness/eating-disorder-statistics.

"Body Image & Eating Disorders," National Eating Disorders Association, accessed April 20, 2020, http://www.nationaleatingdisorders.org/body-image-eating-disorders.

Canadian Population Health Initiative, *Women's Health Surveillance Report: A Multi-dimensional Look at the Health of Canadian Women* (Ottawa: Canadian Institute for Health Information, 2003), https://secure.cihi.ca/free_products/CPHI_WomensHealth_e.pdf.

Leslie Baxter, Nichole Egbert, and Evelyn Ho, "Everyday Health Communication Experiences of College Students," *Journal of American College Health* 56, no. 4 (January/February 2008): 427.

Chapter 7: Bullying and Sexual Harassment

Canadian Population Health Initiative, *Women's Health Surveillance Report: A Multi-dimensional Look at the Health of Canadian Women* (Ottawa: Canadian Institute for Health Information, 2003), https://secure.cihi.ca/free_products/CPHI_WomensHealth_e.pdf.

"Body Image: Introduction," MediaSmarts, accessed April 20, 2020, https://mediasmarts.ca/body-image/body-image-introduction.

"How Common Is Bullying?", "What Is Bullying?", BullyingCanada, accessed April 30, 2020, https://www.bullyingcanada.ca/get-help/#faq.

Bonnie H. Bowie, "Relational Aggression, Gender, and the Developmental Process," *Journal of Child and Adolescent Psychiatric Nursing* 20, no. 2 (2007): 107–15.

Meda Chesney-Lind, Merry Morash, and Katherine Irwin, "Policing Girlhood? Relational Aggression and Violence Prevention," *Youth Violence and Juvenile Justice* 5, no. 3 (July 2007): 328–45.

"Why Do Some Girls Get Bullied?", "Bullying," girlshealth.gov, updated August 24, 2018, https://www.girlshealth.gov/bullying/whybullied/index.html.

"How Does Bullying Hurt?", "Bullying," girlshealth.gov, updated September 30, 2014, https://www.girlshealth.gov/bullying/hurt/index.html.

Shaheen Shariff, "Cyber-Dilemmas in the New Millennium: School Obligations to Provide Student Safety in a Virtual School Environment," *McGill Journal of Education* 40, no. 3 (2005): 457–77.

Donna Schoenrock, quoted in Naomi Langford-Wood and Brian Salter, *Dealing with Difficult People in a Week: How to Deal with Difficult People in Seven Simple Steps* (London: John Murray Learning, 2016).

Merriam-Webster, s.v. "sexual harassment," accessed April 20, 2020, https://www.merriam-webster.com/dictionary/sexual%20harassment.

Lee A. Beaty and Erick B. Alexeyev, "The Problem of School Bullies: What the Research Tells Us," *Adolescence* 43 (Spring 2008): 1–11.

Shariff, "Cyber-Dilemmas in the New Millennium," #. [Page number?]

American Psychological Association, Task Force on the Sexualization of Girls, *Report of the APA Task Force on the Sexualization of Girls* (Washington, DC: American Psychological Association, 2007), http://www.apa.org/pi/women/programs/girls/report-full.pdf.

Girls Action Foundation, *Girls in Canada Today: National Opinion Poll and Report on the Status of Girls* (Montréal: Girls Action Foundation, 2011), 3, https://www.yumpu.com/en/document/read/22821299/read-the-full-report-girls-in-canada-today-girls-action-foundation.

Information about Amanda's story and legacy, including her YouTube video, can be found on https://www.amandatoddlegacy.org/.

Girls Action Foundation, *Girls in Canada Today*, 2.

Girls Action Foundation, *Girls in Canada Today*, #. [Page number?]

"How Common Is Bullying?"

"Sexual Harassment: What It Is and How to Cope," Kids Help Phone, accessed April 20, 2020, http://www.kidshelpphone.ca/get-info/sexual-harassment-what-it-and-how-cope.

Chapter 8: Body Image and Self-Esteem

"Body Image and Self-Esteem," "Health Promotion & Prevention," National Eating Disorder Information Centre, accessed April 20, 2020, https://nedic.ca/health-promotion-prevention/.

Josée L. Jarry, Amy Kossert, and Karen Ip, "Do Women with Low Self-Esteem Use Appearance to Feel Better?", National Eating Disorder Information Centre, 2005, https://nedic.ca/download-file/1559158309.199979-69/.

Helene Keery, Kerri Boutelle, Patricia Van Den Berg, and J. Kevin Thompson, "The Impact of Appearance-Related Teasing by Family Members," *Journal of Adolescent Health* 37, no. 2 (2005): 120–27.

"Real Girls, Real Pressure: A National Report on the State of Self Esteem," Dove Self-Esteem Fund, June 2008, http://www.projectdesign-nyc.com/clients/edelman/dove_epk/press/DSEF_Report.pdf.

"Body Image and Self-Esteem."

Daniel Clay, Vivian L. Vignoles, and Helga Dittmar, "Body Image and Self-Esteem among Adolescent Girls: Testing the Influence of Sociocultural Factors," *Journal of Research on Adolescence* 15, no. 4 (November 2005): 473.

Chapter 9: What to Look for in the Media

Kahlil Gibran, "The Sayings of the Brook," *The Third Treasury of Kahlil Gibran* (New York: Open Road Media, 2011).

Hanne Blank, "Real Women," 2011, http://www.hanneblank.com/blog/2011/06/23/real-women/. The original blog post has since been removed, but "Real Women" has been cited on Goodreads (https://www.goodreads.com/author/show/61858.Hanne_Blank), and a recording of Hanne Blank reading her essay is available at Laura M, "Hanne Blank Reads 'Real Women' at Three Big Fat Voices," uploaded June 1, 2013, YouTube video, 2:28, https://www.youtube.com/watch?v=0JjRi2mTI8E.

Chapter 10: Changing How You Think: Ten Steps to Loving Your Body

Fery Le Non, *365 Quotes about Life and Few Less Important Things* (Morrisville, NC: Lulu Press, 2014), #. [Page number?]

ABOUT FAMILIUS

VISIT OUR WEBSITE: WWW.FAMILIUS.COM

Familius is a global trade publishing company that publishes books and other content to help families be happy. We believe that the family is the fundamental unit of society and that happy families are the foundation of a happy life. We recognize that every family looks different, and we passionately believe in helping all families find greater joy. To that end, we publish books for children and adults that invite families to live the Familius Nine Habits of Happy Family Life: love together, play together, learn together, work together, talk together, heal together, read together, eat together, and laugh together. Founded in 2012, Familius is located in Sanger, California.

CONNECT

Facebook: www.facebook.com/paterfamilius
Twitter: @familiustalk, @paterfamilius1
Pinterest: www.pinterest.com/familius
Instagram: @familiustalk

FAMILIUS

The most important work you ever do will be within the walls of your own home.